Carving Jelly

A Managers reference to implementing CRM
(Customer Relationship Management systems)

Nick Siragher

CHILTERN
PUBLISHING INTERNATIONAL

First published 2001 by Chiltern Publishing International Limited

CHILTERN PUBLISHING INTERNATIONAL LIMITED
Westfields, London Road, High Wycombe, Bucks HP11 1HA

© Chiltern Publishing International Ltd   2001

British Library Cataloguing in Publication Data
A CIP catalogue record for this book can be obtained from the British Library

ISBN 0-9540280-0-7

Typeset, printed and bound in Great Britain by
BAS Printers Limited, Stockbridge, Hampshire

Table of Contents

Welcome

Welcome to 'Carving Jelly', so called because like carving jelly, CRM is possible. Sometimes it doesn't seem possible, but it is. It takes careful preparation, the correct mix of ingredients prepared in the right way, and a degree of skill and experience. 'Carving Jelly' represents the distilled knowledge from involvement in numerous CRM projects, in numerous sectors in many countries. Enjoy.

Nick Siragher

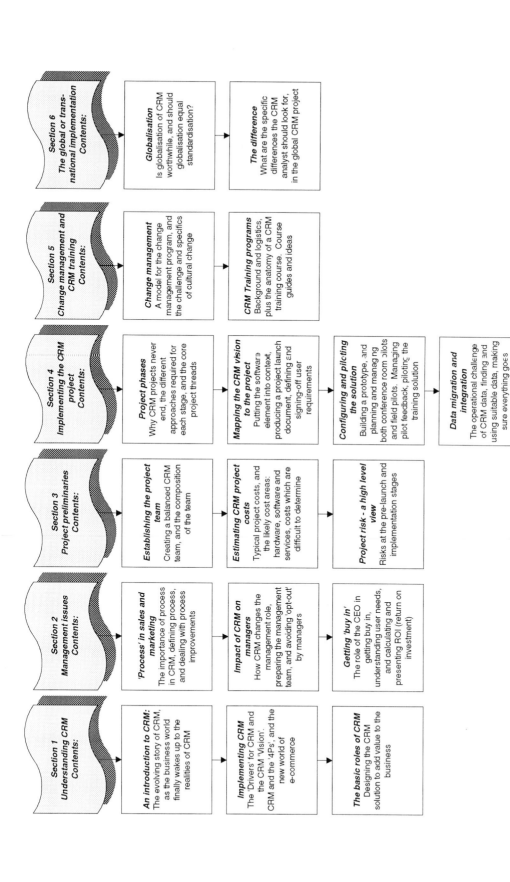

**Section 1
Understanding CRM
Contents:**

An introduction to CRM:
The evolving story of CRM, as the business world finally wakes up to the realities of CRM

Implementing CRM
The 'Drivers' for CRM and the CRM 'Vision'. CRM and the '4Ps', and the new world of e-commerce

The basic roles of CRM
Designing the CRM solution to add value to the business

**Section 2
Management issues
Contents:**

'Process' in sales and marketing
The importance of process in CRM, defining process, and dealing with process improvements

Impact of CRM on managers
How CRM changes the management role, preparing the management team, and avoiding 'opt-out' by managers

Getting 'buy in'
The role of the CEO in getting buy in, understanding user needs, and calculating and presenting ROI (return on investment)

**Section 3
Project preliminaries
Contents:**

Establishing the project team
Creating a balanced CRM team, and the composition of the team

Estimating CRM project costs
Typical project costs, and the likely cost areas: hardware, software and services, costs which are difficult to determine

Project risk - a high level view
Risks at the pre-launch and implementation stages

**Section 4
Implementing the CRM project
Contents:**

Project phases
Why CRM projects never end, the different approaches required for each stage, and the core project threads

Mapping the CRM vision to the project
Putting the software element into context, producing a project launch document, defining and signing-off user requirements

Configuring and piloting the solution
Building a prototype, and planning and managing both conference room pilots and field pilots. Managing pilot feedback, piloting the training solution

Data migration and integration
The operational challenge of CRM data, finding and using suitable data, making sure everything goes smoothly

**Section 5
Change management and CRM training
Contents:**

Change management
A model for the change management program, and the challenge and specifics of cultural change

CRM Training programs
Background and logistics, plus the anatomy of a CRM training course. Course guides and ideas

**Section 6
The global or trans-national implementation
Contents:**

Globalisation
Is globalisation of CRM worthwhile, and should globalisation equal standardisation?

The difference
What are the specific differences the CRM analyst should look for, in the global CRM project

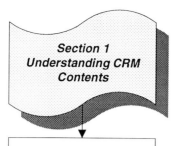

Section 1
Understanding CRM
Contents

An introduction to CRM
The evolving story of
CRM, as the business
world finally wakes up to
the realities of CRM

Implementing CRM
The 'Drivers' for CRM and
the CRM 'Vision'.
CRM and the '4Ps', and
the new world of
e-commerce

The basic roles of CRM
Designing the CRM
solution to add value to
the business

**Section 1
Understanding CRM**

An introduction to CRM
The evolving story of
CRM, as the business
world finally wakes up to
the realities of CRM

This section

Implementing CRM
The 'Drivers' for CRM and
the CRM 'Vision'.
CRM and the '4Ps', and
the new world of
e-commerce

The basic roles of CRM
Designing the CRM
solution to add value to
the business

Section 1 – Background to CRM

Understanding the origin and background to CRM may, through sharing the evolution of what is a relatively new area, help firms understand where CRM fits into their own business. Therefore this section considers the origin of these CRM systems, and the impact of CRM on how firms trade.

The section considers how in the future firms will expect to be sold to, marketed at and provided with customer service. In addition, the section introduces the concept of 'e-commerce', in the context of the traditional 4Ps[1] of marketing.

E-commerce is important because it has recently emerged as one of the most significant aspects of CRM. E-commerce challenges the suitability of the 4Ps to today's business environment. This challenge is because e-commerce incorporates the concept of constantly increasing market segmentation to the point of single customer segments, constantly challenging routes to market to integrate virtual channels and constantly providing the process / system combinations customers demand. Most importantly, e-commerce increases the risk of customer defection, and therefore demands urgent attention.

E-commerce, together with 'seamless integration' to back office systems, should finally lead to the across-the-board adoption of IT in sales marketing and customer service – and the arrival of CRM as a de-facto standard for the normal business model.

The business-to-business community finally wake up to CRM

After a decade of inertia, the business community is now finally waking up to a few realities about corporate life (or death) in the 21st century.

Captains of industry are finally realising that their traditional markets are under threat from firms that care nothing for tradition, or the established way of doing things. Yesterday's airline is tomorrow's banker, last week's Internet start-up is now a mega corporation. Today's world is small, and we are a global business community. The future is here. For many, it arrived early, and caught them sleeping.

Businesses are waking up to realise that their customers are not 'their' customers any more, and that 'their' customers are as disloyal

---

[1]Wilmhurst and IOM, 1986, 'Fundamentals and practices of marketing' ISBN 0 434 923311. The 4Ps concepts have been re-written in many ways, but still serve as a useful common denominator for what is known as 'common marketing theory'.

as they are, when they see a better deal across the street. They are waking up to the revolution in communications, and the information explosion. They are facing the fact that the next decade will make the last 25 years of the 20th century look like the Middle Ages.

Finally, the business community is getting the message that you cannot trade at the speed of light with a horse and cart. To this end, the business community is realising that Marketing, Sales, and Customer relationship management are no longer discrete departmental activities, and that organisations must work <u>cohesively</u> to support the customer. And, at the centre of it all, are Customer Relationship Management systems.

IT in Sales, Marketing and Customer service

Most managers have probably been exposed to some form of 'systemisation' of the Sales, Marketing and Customer Service processes. Such exposure generally falls short of what we now know as 'CRM', but may have provided a glimpse of things to come. And, statistically, many managers will also have participated in 'system failures' in this area. Failures where IT in Sales, Marketing and Customer service has contrived to drive down sales, hinder marketing, and do nothing for Customer Service.

To gauge the success or failure of CRM strategy, consider the strategy in the context of this working definition:

'CRM systems are systems that enable firms to add value to their business by exploiting a better understanding of their customers and markets and associated business processes'.

CRM systems show how a firm uses resources. They provide support for the ever-increasing levels of market segmentation, increasing numbers of routes to market, and provide support for increasingly complex sales and marketing processes, such as those associated with the Internet and similar e-commerce-enabling technologies. They allow a firm to meet the needs of their customers in terms of how the customer wishes to be marketed to, sold to and provided with services.

A less dry and less academic definition would define these systems thus:

'CRM systems are systems that enable firms to apply common sense to the job of sales marketing and customer service. They are enabling systems. They enable smart firms to be smarter, and they enable dumb firms to be dumber'.

The 'system' is only part of the CRM solution. More properly, CRM represents a business strategy; the definition should encompass both the strategic and the operational, and encompass a range of business processes, as outlined below, and provided by Hewson Consulting Limited.

'CRM is a business strategy focused on winning, growing and keeping the right customers'.

The evolutionary story of CRM

In about 1989/90 a few pioneering firms saw the market potential for using technology in sales, marketing and customer service.

'Look!' these pioneering firms cried – 'see how you can organise your marketing in new ways, with the use of new technology'. 'Look!' they yelled – 'you could do the same with your sales process, and your customer service process'. Loudly and triumphantly, they proclaimed the arrival of IT in the sales and marketing office.

CRM systems were finally born (although at the time, the name CRM was 10 years away). That they are still in adolescence is an intriguing part of the evolutionary story. By rights, they should be approaching middle age, but they are not.

The pioneering CRM vendors could see the impact their technical solutions would have. However, what the vendors did not predict was the **downstream** impact their systems would have. The vendors did not predict that the real IT revolution would impact more on those buying than on those selling, and more on those receiving than providing service first.

The vendors failed to predict that because of 'new technology', customer expectations would massively rise, forcing sellers to change the way they sell. The vendors thought that firms would instinctively move to new technologies to support the sales marketing and customer service function *first, with perhaps added benefit for their customer's second*.

Vendors also thought that the benefits of their new technologies were obvious. Unfortunately for the vendors, it would take many years before sales, marketing and customer service managers would see things quite this way.

In reality, few firms have moved voluntarily to implement IT in Sales, Marketing and Customer service. In fact, even a decade on, the 'average' sales, marketing or customer service department is still ambivalent about the use of IT. They take it or leave it, their usage is generally dependent on the presence of an individual, championing the use of such systems. There is still little automatic consensus that the department should be **aggressively** exploiting technology in this area.

What now drives firms towards the new technology are the demands placed on them *by their customers and the perceived adoption of technology by their competitors*. It is the demand side leading the technical evolution in system implementation. It is the demands made on sellers by customers that is pushing the boundaries of IT in Sales Marketing and Customer Service. Customers are pushing firms, kicking and screaming towards new technology, aided by the CRM vendor community.

For the next decade at least, the relentless pace of this 'new' technology is unlikely to stop. Moreover, unless managers can demonstrate plausible CRM strategies and CRM-solution operation the value placed on their organisations by the market will position them as 'technology dinosaurs' And their organisation's share prices be downgraded accordingly.

So CRM is beginning to be entrenched in corporate thinking, and we can see sophisticated models emerging that position CRM within the centre of systems strategy – such as the model proposed by the Hewson Group, and shown below.

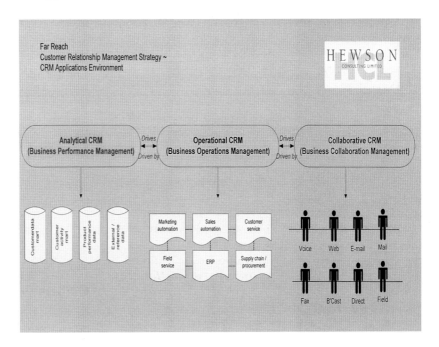

Not surprisingly, the early adopters of IT in sales marketing and customer service were those organisations with the biggest problems, for example, firms with many sales people or complex account management programs or complex distribution channels or those struggling with costly or unwieldy customer service processes. In addition, included as early adopters were firms struggling with their product-based differentiation strategies. These firms found it difficult to differentiate their products from their competitors, and thereby avoid competing solely on price. For such firms, an essential differentiation became service and process efficiency – implemented through new and innovative system solutions.

These early adopters were looking to IT to help gain a significant competitive advantage. They looked to improve performance through process and service efficiencies and, by default, through improved customer segmentation strategies. Today, the term 'e commerce' is in use to describe a combination of these improvement areas – where the implementation of the strategy is, through some use of relevant technologies, to massively improve process efficiencies and massively increase the depth of a firm's segmentation strategy.

What went wrong, and why didn't the current explosion of interest in CRM happen years ago? After all, as a business philosophy CRM does not necessarily need e-commerce as a pre-requisite.

Unfortunately, some early CRM 'experiments' went very wrong. Typically, managers implemented very minimalist system strategies. These strategies often resolved just one issue or addressed just a single process. At the time, the decision to implement these so-called 'point solutions' appeared correct.

Although these managers had complex problems, they opted for simple systems. They made a semi-logical decision, saying 'We know we have a *big* problem – but at the moment we only trust a *small* solution'.

The lack of wholly suitable systems drove managers to apply small tactical solutions to large problems. Some managers were successful and moved through the evolutionary ladder of systems. Most however failed, since their ambitions and plans were too small to address the real issues they faced – and above all, they failed to get CEO level support or to bring the organisation along with them, to face the cultural changes necessary to achieve CRM. ***They implemented operational system strategies where there existed a need for both strategic CRM cultural change and strategic CRM system change.***

Where does 'the buyer' fit, in the evolutionary story of CRM?

Buyers increasingly demand a say in how they are sold to. They expect a higher level of service from more channels, including over the telephone and via the Internet. After all, in the consumer sector, service levels are increasing and business managers are simply consumers in disguise. They expect higher levels of service in their businesses, as they now do in their homes.

These higher-service-level expectations include the 'service' of Marketing, Sales and, more obviously, Customer Service. Buyers want a say in how they are sold to. Buyers want a say in how the seller will present information to them, in what format and at what frequency. Buyers want to choose whether they should go and get information themselves – rather than have it forced on them. Buyers want a say in when the sales representative will (or now more frequently will not) call on them. Buyers want to share in the account-management process.

In short, buyers want treating as the intelligent individuals they generally are. Buyers want mature relationships, sharing information freely and correctly between buyer and seller.

Correspondingly, the old days of selling by persuasion, over logical argument are long gone and, likely, never to return. There is little room left for the fast-talking silver-tongued sales person. Intelligence is winning over charisma, as information becomes the new persuader. This doesn't mean there is no need for sales people – far from it. It simply means that now, the sales person has to be ever smarter, ever more knowledgeable, and ever more resilient, as do his or her colleagues in marketing and customer service. Because, with information so readily available, the scope for Sales and Marketing to add value diminishes.

It is in this context that firms should be looking at IT in Sales, Marketing and Customer Service. They should be looking to see how new technology could provide a higher level of customer service, right along the customer / prospect value chain. A concept that proponents of Porter's 'value chain' will appreciate.

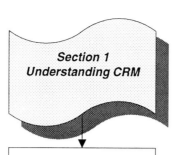

Section 1
Understanding CRM

An introduction to CRM
The evolving story of
CRM, as the business
world finally wakes up to
the realities of CRM

Implementing CRM
The 'Drivers' for CRM and
the CRM 'Vision'.
CRM and the '4Ps', and
the new world of
e-commerce

This section

The basic roles of CRM
Designing the CRM
solution to add value to
the business

The drivers for implementing a CRM solution

Vision

No CRM project is going to get off the ground without a vision and a visionary leader – a leader committed to championing the project from start to finish. The 'vision thing', therefore, is about visioning how the organisation is to position itself against the key drivers to implement a CRM strategy.

After that, the organisation can face the practical issues of working out how to pay for the new system, and the nuts and bolts of 'getting buy in', and planning and implementing the project. The first part therefore of this section is about creating the CRM vision. That is, articulating the vision to the management team, and making sure everyone understands what the drivers are for an investment in this area. The second part of this section is about planning to achieve the vision, starting with getting 'buy in' from the management team.

'The vision thing' is important, because firms must decide how to respond to the massive changes currently underway in the world of business-to-business sales, marketing, and customer-relationship management. *Solving tactical issues, with new system process combinations will help – but, by definition, only in the short term*.

So what exactly is going on? What is it that makes market analysts the world over claim the CRM market as *'billions of dollars each year and rising'*? Rising to trillions that is, if you add in the related 'e-commerce' expenditure. Why are the world's largest (and smallest) consultancies gearing up for an explosion of CRM work and e-commerce work? Why are they continuing to drive forward their ERP practices – driving them forward towards UBS practices? (Universal Business Solution.)

If one claimed a single answer to this question it would definitely be the wrong one. The right answer concerns a combination of factors, all occurring at or around the same time, relating to the IT revolution, where the IT revolution is a driver for the globalisation of business, and the driver towards the 'single customer' marketing segment.

Massive and revolutionary changes

The diagram over-simplifies what are massive and revolutionary changes caused by the IT revolution in the way in which the world does business. By changing the speed at which firms *could* do business, IT led the revolution.

Using increased processing power, firms could both develop and market products at an ever-increasing rate. In addition, IT enabled firms

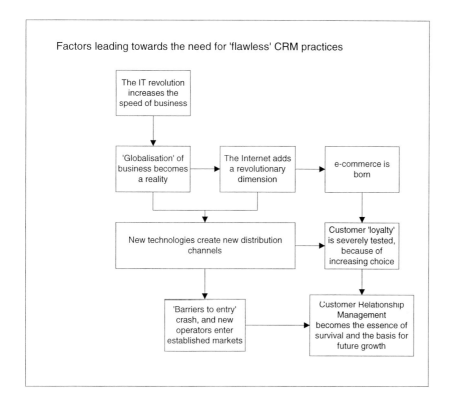

Factors leading towards the need for 'flawless' CRM practices

The IT revolution increases the speed of business

'Globalisation' of business becomes a reality

The Internet adds a revolutionary dimension

e-commerce is born

New technologies create new distribution channels

Customer 'loyalty' is severely tested, because of increasing choice

'Barriers to entry' crash, and new operators enter established markets

Customer Relationship Management becomes the essence of survival and the basis for future growth

to become 'global' – by providing the necessary technical links between operating companies. These technical links enabled firms to remove the traditional barriers to globalisation – time and distance. In addition, the growth of global standards for operating systems and software applications supported the administrative needs of the global business. It became possible to do business anywhere, anytime, almost as if at home. Of course cultural barriers prevailed, but not infrastructure barriers.

At the same time, the Internet revolutionised the way in which individuals wanted to receive (and corporations provided) information. This combination of technologies enabled firms to do two things.

Firstly, to establish a diversity of distribution channels. This became possible as IT in general enabled firms to create a tighter bond with their partners, and the Internet made 'virtual' trading relatively acceptable – i.e. the concept of location as an important factor diminished. Some firms moved towards disintermediation, others took an alternative view, and found new markets through new and innovative distribution channels.

Currently, e-commerce is beginning to thrive in this environment. Undoubtedly it will continue to thrive as a practical reality to exploit the connected world, and provide the ever greater degrees of service needed to capture, maintain, and develop customers – a must in the increasingly competitive world.

As a result, the traditional concepts of 'barriers to entry' changed – the virtual world being quicker, cheaper, and easier to enter, than the real world. In addition, the basis of survival became CRM as much as product innovation. The result is that now, now in the post-revolutionary world, firms must create 'flawless' CRM as a pre-requisite to survival or prosperity. *And the challenge is on to keep customers loyal.*

The critical need for 'flawless' CRM – customer loyalty, the ultimate CRM business drivers

To operate in this 'post revolutionary world' the organisation must be clear about its response to three critical aspects of the business *relating to customer loyalty:*

1) *the threat from new entrants*, primarily those being able to enter the market at low cost, incredibly quickly
2) *the introduction of e-commerce*
3) *changes to the distribution channel*, as a result of the impact of other contemporary changes.

There are undoubtedly other challenges. But these three constantly emerge as being the most important drivers to implement CRM strategy. Remembering, of course, that customer loyalty in the context of CRM means keeping the customers the firm wishes to keep and jettisoning the rest.

The threat from new entrants
In the old days – about 18 months ago (!) – new entrants had to get up and running at least to the same speed as the incumbent operator; then launch, then operate, then become a threat. In the meantime, the incumbents could watch this entire process, and plan their strategies accordingly.

That was then. This is now.
Now, we can bank with our airline, buy our holidays with the weekly ham, and get medical advice on platform 7 – whilst waiting for a train. Admittedly, these are all consumer-based examples, not business to business. However, where consumer markets go with regard to service levels, business-to-business has a habit of following.

Example – Buying a PC Network

Change happens at mega speed. Not long ago if you wanted a PC network for a small business you would call in a few consultants, track down some suppliers, go out to tender, wait for ages and then get the system installed. It would not work, but at least you had the system.

Now, if you want a small business network (or even a large business network) go to www.dell.com (or similar) and get it from the comfort of your office. Of course, it still may not work…but that is another issue! Actually, it is not another issue. Suppliers now fix things quickly and at a low cost, from a distance. Even the 'not working' problem is less of a problem now than it ever was.

The example demonstrates that if there is a faster, lower cost, higher-value proposition method to deliver something, there is someone out there looking to do so. Accordingly, a rigorous analysis of existing barriers to entry is important, along with the potential to be deconstructed or become a deconstructor – discussed below.

The introduction of e-commerce

In the business-to-business world, e-commerce is not necessarily about buying something over the Internet, for example a book, some software or a flight. E-commerce is about changing the way customers see us, and how we see our customers. It is about giving customers access to everything the customer needs, to support the customer relationship. Notice the terminology – *giving customers access…* it means letting customers into systems to help themselves to what they need, to make their businesses run more smoothly and more profitably.

For example, e-commerce is about providing 'price and delivery' information, on line. It is about allowing customers to order online. It is about letting customers check their account status on line and access whatever they want, electronically, whenever they want. And doing the same with prospective customers and channel partners and suppliers. It is about being brave enough to let go of the 'us and them' culture, so ingrained in numerous organisations, right along their value chain. If your firm sells pumps or cranes or chemicals or tractors or whatever (i.e. whatever most people wouldn't dream of anyone buying over the web) don't think that e-commerce is not for your organisation. Think instead about every single customer interaction. Think about how to provide information, and how to support customers (and prospective customers and suppliers), and how much of that might move to an electronic format.

With regard to e-commerce, the question every pundit is now asking is this. How long will e-commerce provide *a competitive advantage*, and when, sector-by-sector, will it become a necessity? This, of course, is not a new question for such a scenario. Nevertheless, it needs answering. As a minimum, firms should know the e-commerce trends in their own sector, since e-commerce is soon to sit at the heart of the business-to-business organisation's CRM strategy. Following on from this, it is necessary to understand what time remains to complete the strategy, to either stay on par, or move ahead of the competition. And don't be surprised if the results of this analysis are frightening. They probably will be. Soon we must lose the 'e' from e-Commerce and just accept that 'e' is how Commerce works.

Example: Electronic Controls company

An established player in the electronic controls business thought their strong personal relationships with their customers would keep out the international competitors. They believed that if competitors began to encroach on 'their' markets, they would have at least 18 months' notice – seemingly more than enough time to adopt an appropriate competitive response. After all, they argued, it had taken 15 years to get to their current position.

A competitor managed to take significant market share in just 6 months. Using only a skeleton UK presence, the competitor established a web presence, and insisted on handling all enquiries by telephone, and via their extensive web site. Whilst this did not suit all buyers, it suited enough buyers to capture market share, and change this section of the electronic controls business.

The new player deconstructed a critical and profitable section of the market, leaving the incumbents to fight over the rest.

Changes to the distribution channel

Firms collaborate more than ever, especially where their products and services are complex, and require a diverse range of skills to deliver to the end user. So the adage that 'nobody goes to market alone' becomes increasingly true.

However, with the growth of CRM there is a range of factors that impact on those that sell through a distribution channel:

1. The delivery route for knowledge is changing in favour of the virtual route. This virtual route is managed directly by the originator of knowledge. Therefore, the traditional role of a 'knowledge partner' in the distribution channel is changing, and the importance of where knowledge is held in the channel also changes.

2. New CRM technologies provide firms with a chance to consider who really 'owns' the customer, and affords better opportunities for ownership if they wish.

3. Contemporary changes are forcing firms to undertake careful consideration of ROI (Return on Investment) on the effectiveness of their channel strategies. Not least, the emergence of new options for channel forces the evaluation of existing channel strategies.

The prediction is that over the next 5 years routes to market will go through a radical transformation. Therefore, these issues are discussed in more depth below:

The importance of where knowledge is held in the channel – and knowledge disintermediation

The Internet makes it less critical that the distributor has all the answers required by the customer. Through the Internet, firms are able to disintermediate much of the knowledge associated with customer acquisition and servicing. This leaves the channel, predominantly, to pick up the practical aspects of taking the order, delivering, and taking care of the physical side of the after-market. For simplicity, this could be known as '*knowledge disintermediation*', where partners are selected for *what they do*, not *how they think* – their job being to apply knowledge owned by the principal. The extension of knowledge disintermediation is that from the perspective of the principal, the choice of channel partner widens. This is because the selection criterion places the scarce resource of knowledge lower down the list.

Knowledge disintermediation will be the biggest thing to shake up selling through a channel since the invention of the telephone. Such wider choice of channel partner (i.e. where the partner doesn't need so much knowledge) makes the existing channel sharper, making it fight harder to justify its slice of margin. In turn, this will either increase profits or drive down prices, depending on the industry sector and scenario.

CRM is enabling firms to truly 'own' its customers

Channel partners rarely allow their principals unfettered access to what they see as 'their' customers. However, with the introduction of more powerful CRM solutions it becomes ever easier for the principals to identify 'their' customers. Once identified, principals can choose to build some form of direct relationship – direct that is, in contrast to the indirect relationships established, and maintained through brand-management strategies and activity-supporting channel partners.

Once a principal knows who the channel partners' customers are, what they buy, how they behave etc, the power relationship between principal and partner changes. The IT revolution and flawless CRM provide such an understanding. Correspondingly, this understanding is likely to change the shape of the distribution channel, in even the most established markets.

Principals, once fearful of de-stabilising channel partners, can reclaim some of the ground and control lost in recent years. Now, through the application of new technology, the balance of power is shifting towards a more even keel. We can expect to see more ownership of customers at principal level, and less hoarding of customers by distributors.

The costs of operating a distribution channel becomes apparent

The costs of running a distribution channel, versus going direct to market, are difficult to calculate – as is the benefit of switching to or from either model. This is especially so where a direct and channel sales operation run in parallel. At the same time, the new channel options afforded by CRM, and the Internet, mean it has never been more critical than now to know how much the channel really costs to operate or how much benefit it really provides. Armed with this knowledge, managers are in a far better position to develop their channel strategies (i.e. use channels or go direct).

Deconstruction

A factor which complicates the 'customer loyalty / customer retention' debate is the 'deconstruction' factor.

Deconstruction refers to the practice of deconstructing a competitor or an industry sector. The 'deconstructor' finds the most valuable part of a business or sector, and sets up shop to exploit specifically this area. The business is taken generally by an 'e'-based approach.

Two things make this deconstruction possible. Firstly, the adoption of standards and secondly, the richness of information abounding in the electronic world. With standards, buyers can be sure of what they are getting. With enough information, buyers can make considered purchases, and are becoming increasingly inclined so to do, with little direct reference to sellers.

Example: The retail car business

A good example of 'deconstruction' is the passenger car business. The expensive and high effort part of the business is establishing and managing the showroom, and managing an inventory. Selling cars over the web – and only over the web – removes these costs. More importantly, it exploits the incumbents who continue to act as showrooms for the Internet players – for example, the move by the Virgin organisation into car retailing via the web. The same applies to white goods and TV and audio equipment. Of course, these are all consumer-based examples, but it won't be long before business-to-business examples abound.

Alternatively, we may see a continuance of the 'bricks and mortar' companies rising to the challenge of the new deconstructing Internet-centric operations. Expect to see traditional firms, dented by 'e'-based decontructors fighting back with their own 'e'-based operations. They may yet be successful, given that the established players have 'brand' and a customer base on their side. However, whatever happens, firms will continue to isolate profitable parts of businesses and target them accordingly.

Whatever happened to the 4Ps?

– and an introduction to 'e-commerce' as part of the CRM strategy, in the context of the business drivers for CRM.

At the same time as some Sales Marketing and Customer Service managers are just waking up to IT, something more fundamental is happening in their environment, specifically to the 4Ps. Of course, the term 4Ps is used very loosely, and describes a past way of thinking about marketing theory. Now, many marketing theorists add various other 'Ps' and present theories based on the original concept.

In the past, the manipulation of the 4Ps of marketing (Product, Price, Place, and Promotion) helped to manage and extend product life-cycles. Correspondingly, the 4Ps were the foundation of sales and marketing processes. They were the bedrock of most sales and marketing departments, of marketing training, and just about everything anyone could ever think of on the subject of marketing.

However, the speed of doing business has increased several-fold since the introduction of the 4Ps. The knock-on effect is that product life cycles have collapsed in their traditional form. The 4Ps cannot now support product differentiation so effectively, at least in their traditional application, at the speed that markets now change. What was once a five-yearly product cycle reduces to a yearly product cycle. Yearly product cycles reduce to quarterly cycles. In some sectors, the product life-cycle is now so short it is simply a matter of weeks before competitors imitate a new product. The once innovative product rapidly moves towards 'commodity' status as differentiators vanish under a fusillade of 'me too' products.

At the same time, new channels emerge, not least the Internet and the integrated use of the telephone. New channels emerge in the shape of 'virtual companies' – loose associations or networks of like-minded firms joining forces to take a slice of whatever action they can. These channels are held together by the string of new technology – e-mail and the World Wide Web. Channels that the originators of the 4Ps could not possibly have imagined.

Now, there is no longer a 'level playing field' or a single set of shared rules and values. Witness the revolution in banking or airlines – changed beyond recognition by new entrants who make their own rules.

Because of this ever-changing landscape, few firms can rely solely on such an outdated concept as the 4Ps. After all, can we really expect a 1960s' concept to apply 40 years on? What a nice (romantic yet naïve) thought, i.e. a concept that was good when '*we never had it so good*' is still good today. Surely not?

Successful firms take what they want from 4Ps thinking. However, successful firms now also choose to differentiate **by improved processes, and effective management of customer relationships** and by exploiting a myriad of innovative channels and ideas. They take knowledge management and 'e-business' in their stride.

In doing all this, they compensate for the reduced power of the once 'all-powerful' 4Ps. In practice, compensating for the reduced power of the 4Ps requires the introduction of powerful CRM and e-commerce solutions and, to understand this, it is necessary to have an insight into the practicalities of e-commerce.

E-commerce in the context of CRM

E-commerce is a reflection of the need to gain advantage through channel optimisation and process differentiation, via the use of the Internet. For example, if a customer wants to know if something is in stock – why make them call up and find out? Why not let them into the stock systems, to look for themselves? The same applies to account queries and product advice, and a whole range of related processes. This is just one small example of the practical application of e-commerce.

In practice, e-commerce requires firms to join forces, **buyers and sellers electronically integrating their processes and systems** to mutual benefit – so e-commerce is not simply buying and selling over the Internet. This part of the IT revolution is much more than that. An explosion of information management systems and knowledge-centric business cultures is driving this revolution.

Buyers now frequently know more than sellers. Therefore, in accepting e-commerce and the corresponding knowledge and information explosion, we must accept that the age of the 'intelligent buyer' is with us. We must see intelligent buyers as today's *majority*, where they were yesterday's *minority*. Their intelligence pushes them towards exploiting the obvious benefits of e-commerce. The most obvious benefit being that e-commerce gives sales, marketing, and customer service managers the opportunity to provide the services their customers demand, and revolutionise their thinking. Now, their customers can be as demanding as they like, since theoretically the systems are / soon will be in place to deliver.

With product differentiation more difficult than ever and established channel strategies under threat, the new battleground is becoming a 'process'. Which makes 'process' the new differentiator.

By extension it follows that where all things are equal (products, prices and service levels), an important differentiator then becomes ***how well one firm can integrate their processes into another firm's process and thereby engender customer loyalty – on a scale never seen before.***

For example:

- Global couriers (e.g. TNT, DHL) allow all their customers, via the Internet, to request a package collection, track a package during the delivery or query an invoice. Some customers integrate further, with automated invoice payment to the courier, in exchange for preferential terms
- Fuel suppliers (e.g. BP, Mobil) have for years offered 'fuel cards' to their customers with fleets of cars. In addition, they now integrate their billing process directly into their customers' management accounts. This enables their customers to track usage in their own terms – not in the terms of the organisation supplying the fuel
- Hotels offering corporate services (for example global chains offering training and conference rooms, Forte, Holiday Inn, Sheraton) automatically import their clients' training schedules into their reservation systems – handling conference-room enquiries at record-breaking speeds

Each of these companies would be likely to admit that, at face value, their product is not so different from those of their competitors. These firms differentiate through supporting their brands, and by attempting to outwit their competitors as their markets evolve. Nevertheless, their product offerings are fundamentally similar. Yet each company manages to differentiate beyond their basic 'commodity' products.

Aside from supporting their brands, one of the ways in which these firms differentiate is through their ability to integrate their processes, with those processes of their customers as outlined above. At the same time, these firms use IT to help segment different (or rather new) customer segments, and develop new processes specifically for these customer segments. They can do so because they have 'solved' CRM and solved 'process integration' right along their value chain.

What is the starting point for process integration?

Process integration does not happen overnight. Firms must work hard to be in a position to discuss process integration with their partners. In addition, firms must understand their own processes sufficiently well. And, for many, this is the first obstacle.

Repeatedly, we see there is a common factor in process-integrated organisations. Well-integrated organisations already have a history of superior customer relationship-management (achieved before CRM became popular). These organisations know their customers. These organisations use their long-held knowledge to predict their customers' needs. Above all, they think in terms of managing the 'relationship process' above 'managing the account'. They think holistically about relationship management as part of a wider business process. They stopped thinking sequentially long ago, i.e. where account management is simply a number of steps to complete, in a given time period, to achieve the quarterly target.

These cultures are ones in which the traditional 'silo' thinking between Sales, Marketing and Customer Service no longer exists.

In developing the 'process-integrated' organisation, we now see that both e-commerce and CRM are not simply about the technology that joins the process-integrated organisations. It is more fundamental than that.

It is about using these enabling technologies to enable massive cultural changes. The change is necessary to break down the 'us' and 'them' barriers between buyers and sellers –an essential pre-requisite to process integration – and of course break down barriers within the traditional 'silos' of sales, marketing, and customer service.

Firms begin their process-integration strategies with one small step.

That step is realising that, to survive, there are few options other than to **_actively manage_** the customer relationship – and get 'process integrated' with their customers before their competitors do. And to do that, they have to challenge organisational thinking away from the silo mentality, and move towards the CRM mentality.

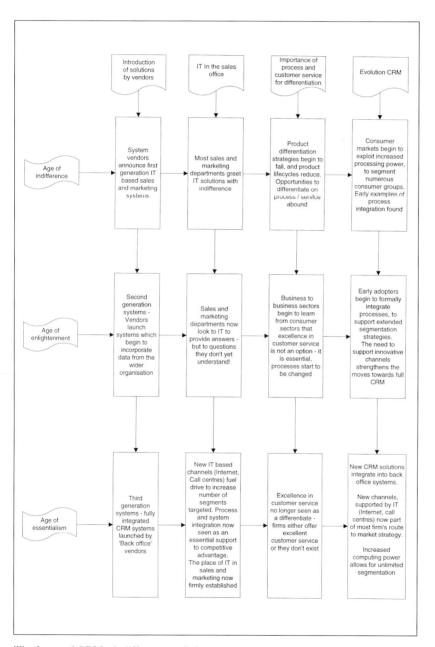

The 3 ages of CRM – indifference, enlightenment and essentialism

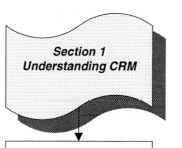

Section 1
Understanding CRM

An introduction to CRM
The evolving story of
CRM, as the business
world finally wakes up to
the realities of CRM

Implementing CRM
The 'Drivers' for CRM and
the CRM 'Vision'.
CRM and the '4Ps', and
the new world of
e-commerce

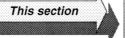

This section

The basic roles of CRM
Designing the CRM
solution to add value to
the business

Introduction

The previous section outlined the high-level business drivers and the fact that, in the future, success for business-to-business firms will depend on the firm's ability to integrate its processes with its customers' processes, and to seek customer loyalty from a desirable customer set.

To position themselves to achieve this, successful firms will be obsessive about understanding the holistic approach to relationship management. Such an holistic approach means seeing the relationship management process as a long-term amalgam of people, products and values, expressed through shared processes and systems.

And to achieve success, firms must maintain flawless systems, which amongst other things will enable them to track their customers' buying cycles, lifetime values, and contact relationships.

These successful firms will know precisely how to pitch their CRM systems relative to their customers' needs. They will understand that the CRM system must be *'Customer-Centric'* rather than *'Supplier-Centric'*. And be at the centre of their sales and marketing operation – not a periphery activity to dip into from time to time.

They will also recognise the importance of having systems that help predict the future, rather than simply report on the past.

All of this requires the business-to-business operation to understand the role of the CRM strategy. Therefore, this section examines the six main roles of CRM:

Role 1 – Be customer- not supplier-centric
Role 2 – Be predictive
Role 3 – Directly support customer retention
Role 4 – Measure in market context, specifically to add value
Role 5 – Support processes
Role 6 – Measure customer value

CRM Role 1 – 'Customer-Centric' not 'Supplier-Centric'

To understand customer needs requires an appreciation of the customers' buying cycle (amongst, of course, many other things). With this understanding, it is possible to define a CRM solution around the customer – a 'customer-centric' solution. This 'customer-centric approach' is in contrast to the 'supplier-centric approach' – where the system user is the 'Supplier', and the system is designed to meet supplier needs first and customer needs second (if at all).

The following examples illustrate the importance of creating customer-centric systems over supplier-centric systems:

- Before designing a supplier-centric system to count how many sales visits representatives complete in a day, design a customer-centric system to record how many purchase decisions customers (and competitors' customers) make each year. The system should also record when they make these purchase decisions.
- From the customer-centric system, use knowledge of customer buying behaviour to get sales people in the right place at the right time, ready to influence the customer. It is then possible to distinguish between when the firm is not getting orders because there are no orders to be had, and when they are not getting orders because there is something more fundamentally wrong.
- Before investing in a complex 'opportunity'-based sales forecasting system, model the relationships between customers and the customer-service team. Understanding this relationship should provide an understanding of why some customers defect to other suppliers. Tracking potential losses helps to protect the existing market share, which is usually easier and costs less than gaining a new market share from a competitor.

The problem with the supplier-centric approach is its isolation relative to the customer. The supplier-centric approach tells firms what happened (if they are lucky) in the context of their own organisation. However, to succeed, it is necessary to know what happened in the context of the customer and therefore set the understanding in the context of the wider market.

So in summary, 'supplier-centric' systems are inward-looking systems, ideal for navel gazing and the like. More effective, and a better model for CRM, are outward-looking customer-centric systems.

CRM Role 2 – Be predictive

History is yesterday's story. Today, we need accurate predictions about tomorrow.

Today, most firms should understand tomorrow's world. For example, tracking what sales people did yesterday only tells you what happened yesterday. Tracking completed marketing campaigns only tells you what happened relative to the campaign process.

The correct role of the CRM system should be to highlight what did happen, **_and then help determine what may or should happen next_**. Firms are then able to consider the responses they should prepare, based on past history, and consider projections for the future. In this way, the CRM solution should be a 'predictive system'.

> *Predictive CRM systems enable extrapolation of past history to help predict the future. They are superior to CRM systems that tell you something when it is too late to do anything about it.*

CRM Role 3 – Directly support customer retention

Customers demand that their suppliers maintain good systems and processes. Unfortunately, they do not do this explicitly. They do it implicitly, by staying loyal to suppliers with good quality processes – and deserting those with poor quality processes.

Consider the following examples, these show system / process combinations to support specific segments and situations. These firms achieve a high degree of loyalty in markets which many would consider simply 'commodity markets'. Markets where price often wins over loyalty, however much these firms achieve loyalty through process integration.

■ A bulk chemical's company maintains the past order history for their key accounts. When the customers' order pattern changes, the supplier notifies the customer – in case the customer has made an error in ordering. For 95% of the time there is no error and all is OK. However, for 5% of the time the supplier saves the customer from running out of stock, and incurring a costly interruption to production. To achieve this level of customer service requires complex integration of sales order processing and sales history files, and close working between customer and supplier. In a commodity-based market, such integration serves as a valuable differentiator and directly supports customer retention. (A fine example of process integration.)

■ A hotel chain stores the detail relating to its customers' annual conferences and events. Months in advance, the hotel chain reminds the customer to begin planning accommodation for these events. Far from finding this intrusive, the customer thanks the hotel by remaining loyal (where booking circumstances permit) even when the clients' personnel change, the system knows that someone in the client company should be booking conference accommodation. The hotel then reminds the client to do so.

■ A corporate-car rental firm notifies its clients when it may benefit the client to buy rather than lease a vehicle, or switch to a different rental rate. This may seem like poor business practice – telling your customer to stop buying something from you and /or buy something that costs less! However, the car-rental firm calculates that, though they may lose a few hires or leases, the long-term pay-off is in increased customer retention, which is a much greater reward.

Understanding the relationship with a client, on a client-by-client basis, requires both complex sales analysis systems, and an understanding of the unique usage pattern of each client. These examples show how some firms share this understanding with their customers. In addition, the information is available where needed, often right in the hands of the Account Manager or Customer Service department. Moreover, the information is set in the context of the market, adding a further and important dimension to the level of understanding. Hence, the solution supports customer retention through process integration.

CRM Role 4 – Measure in 'market context' specifically to add value

Measurement must be relative to the organisation as a whole, and directly in the context of the markets in which the firm operates. The contemporary role of the CRM system, therefore, is to measure exclusively in a way that adds value to the business, i.e., not just measuring for an internal purpose, but measuring to retain and/or increase market share.

There are therefore two simple rules for Role 4:

1. The measurement must be in the context of the market
2. Measurement activity must specifically add value to the business, for example by helping managers protect or increase market share

CRM Role 5 – Support processes

Because processes fail, not people
In general, processes fail people; people do not fail. The problem with attempting to measure what people do (and thereby what they fail at) is that you engender a 'blame' culture. If something goes wrong, the organisation looks to the measurement statistics to prove who or what made it go wrong. Having blamed someone, life can go on.

- Not enough enquiries? – *blame* marketing, they carried out too few campaigns

- Not enough new customers? – *blame* sales, not enough sales activity
- Not enough high-value long-term customers? – *blame* customer services, they upset the best customers

The knee-jerk blame culture produces knee-jerk reactionary solutions. Unfortunately, these solutions occasionally provide only short-term relief to the original problem. Therefore, in the eyes of the problem solvers, they have 'succeeded'. They act, and the problem appears to go away:

- Marketing carry out more campaigns – and get more enquiries as a result
- Sales are more active – and get more customers
- Customer services make a special effort – and stem customer defections

In the short term, the solution removes the symptoms but the illness remains.

Thus, the role of CRM should be to support the development of **efficient end-to-end business processes**. Not simply highlight failings in discrete activities.

CRM Role 6 – Measure 'Customer Value'

All customers like their suppliers to value them. Suppliers generally ensure that they treat big customers as big customers and small customers as small customers. If they get this wrong, the suppliers' 'profitability per account ratio' will be incorrect, and their business will suffer.

The problem of treating customers according to their value is two-fold. Firstly, how to accurately identify the value of a customer. Secondly, how to implement processes that reflect the value of the customer.

To consider the 'correct application' of CRM requires some understanding of what typically goes wrong when managing account profitability. Below are some examples:

- To ensure they treat big accounts as big accounts, numerous firms implement 'Key Account' programs. In these programs, the top accounts are singled out for special status and therefore for special treatment. Common errors in these programs are that firms cannot accurately identify which of them should be in the list of top accounts – although they believe they can – i.e. they think they are right, but are not. For example, judging a key account by past performance simply reflects the top accounts in the context of *the supplier*. This takes no account of firms that may have enormous potential, but only buy a small amount through the supplier and then source the rest elsewhere. When this occurs, an account with major potential is discriminated against (e.g. excluded from the 'A' list) and, naturally enough, is destined to remain a small account forever – since it receives none of the attention enjoyed by the 'top' accounts.

- Some firms segmenting 'top accounts' by volume find their margins collapse. This is because the reason the accounts remain 'top accounts' is that they receive preferential terms. By definition, these accounts are not the most profitable accounts. Worse still, the profitable accounts become neglected, since they are not treated as well as the 'top accounts'. Subsequently, the higher margin firms defect to other suppliers, which erodes the overall margin still further – a dangerous downward spiral.

- A third common error is to concentrate too favourably on the top accounts, at the expense of other accounts. Firms develop complex processes for retaining and developing their top accounts. In the meantime, they treat all other accounts almost as an inconvenience. In revenue and profit terms, the short-term impact may be minor. However, in the long term the smaller accounts defect. This defection leaves few accounts to develop to replace natural wastage in the top accounts. With high quality CRM solutions, the potential exists to manage all accounts *as preferred by the account*.

If firms measure 'customer value' correctly in the first place, there is much more likelihood of providing the correct level of service to customers – which is why, indirectly, firms demand that you measure their value. If you measure their value correctly and act fairly and accordingly there is much more likelihood of retaining the account.

Hence Role 6 of the CRM solution is to manage customer value.

Summary – the role of the CRM solution

CRM solutions should be customer-centric, and predictive and their output based on an intimate understanding of buyer behaviour – relative to the approach to sales marketing and customer service – and market conditions.

The diagram below shows the main roles and positioning of the solution. In this diagram, roles refer to the tasks / processes the solution should support. Positioning refers to how the role is to be implemented.

For example, the role of the system is to 'provide an understanding of buyer and market behaviour'; the position the system takes must be 'Customer- and market- centric'. Armed with such systems, firms can make proper user of today's technology and position resources accordingly, and identify the necessary business processes.

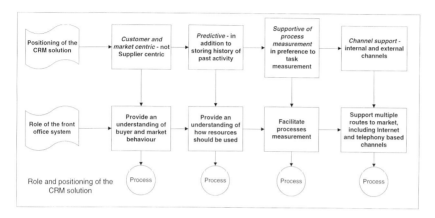

Understanding the role of the CRM solution

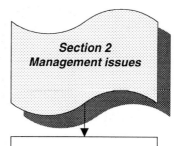

**Section 2
Management issues**

'Process' in sales and marketing
The importance of process in CRM, defining process, and dealing with process improvements

---

Impact of CRM on managers
How CRM changes the management role, preparing the management team, and avoiding 'opt-out' by managers

---

Getting 'buy in'
The role of the CEO in getting buy in, understanding user needs, and calculating and presenting ROI (return on investment)

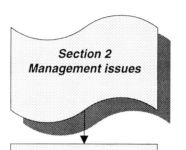

Section 2
Management issues

This section →

'Process' in sales and marketing
The importance of process in CRM, defining process, and dealing with process improvements

Impact of CRM on managers
How CRM changes the management role, preparing the management team, and avoiding 'opt-out' by managers

Getting 'buy in'
The role of the CEO in getting buy in, understanding user needs, and calculating and presenting ROI (return on investment)

Section 2 – Management issues

This section considers the impact of the CRM solution in the context of three key management issues:

- The business processes associated with CRM
- The impact of CRM on the role of managers
- Getting buy-in from the management team

The concept of 'process' – and why it is central to the CRM strategy

Introduction

'Process' is a natural concept for the many parts of a business. But process is not one readily discussed in sales and marketing. Manufacturing is able to produce detailed diagrams showing how the manufacturing process works. Accounts are able to do the same with the billing process and the credit-control process. Distribution will readily show the processes enabling the on-time delivery of goods. In contrast, sales people rarely have process diagrams for closing a deal. And rarer still are process diagrams for implementing market-segmentation strategies. This is not a criticism, simply a statement of fact.

Why don't sales and marketing managers 'do' Process?

For many Sales and Marketing Managers (less so Customer Service Managers), process is like getting a speeding fine or having bad breath – 'process' is something that happens to others. They may even suggest that process is nothing to do with the real business of selling or marketing. Often (though accepting it is dangerous to generalise) they see an evaluation of 'process' as a soft option in their hard competitive world.

There are some specific reasons for the lack of process thinking in sales and marketing. Compared to other departments, these reasons are part historic and partly to do with the nature of sales and marketing;

- The history is that other departments implemented their computer systems over the last 10-30 years or so. For example accounts, purchasing, payroll etc. To achieve their systems, these departments had to write down their business processes – this being necessary to enable the IT people to do their job and produce the required systems. Sales, Marketing and Customer Service departments are just starting out on the IT trail, and the need to write down what they do is only just beginning, evolving since the late 1980s.

- In Sales and Marketing there are few 'best practices' to follow,[2] when compared to other departments. Whether something is done correctly or incorrectly is judged by output relative to input, i.e. the output of revenue or margin, against the input of sales and marketing costs. Rarely, however, is performance judged by how the job is done (i.e. judgement by process performance) or effectiveness.

- Except for some notable industry exceptions[3] there are few legal requirements to record the process of selling or the process of marketing. In contrast (for example), accounting must keep detailed records and store these for several years.

Why is 'process' so important to CRM strategy and CRM solution implementation?

The definition of process is essential to the successful implementation of any computer-based system. Without an understanding of what the process is (or rather should be) there can be no new solution.

In addition, having identified process as a differentiator, and a necessary component of the integrated CRM / e-commerce strategy, it is essential to understand where process thinking fits in terms of the overall CRM strategy. Moreover, as firms integrate processes between each other, this too is a driver for Sales and Marketing managers to understand their processes, as *intuitively as they might understand running a campaign, qualifying a prospect, or closing a deal*.

What happens when managers leave process thinking solely to solution implementers?

Unfortunately, many managers are happy to leave 'process' to the IT department, to the management consultants and the CRM system vendors. For these people process is everything. Process is the stuff that fills their hearts and mind and souls day in and day out. Cut into the flesh of an IT person, management consultant, or system vendor, and out will pour not blood, but process diagrams. The bigger the cut, the more complicated and incomprehensible the diagram.

---

[2] A notable exception is the work of Hewson Consulting Group in this area. In conjunction with Price Waterhouse Coopers, the management consultancy, Hewson run a Sales Process Benchmarking group. See www.hewson.co.uk

[3] For example, the UK financial services sector is heavily legislated, requiring firms to follow guidelines in selling to their customers and record that they follow these guidelines. The pharmaceutical sector requires marketing departments to record the value of promotional material given to prospects and customers. Each of these sectors use IT extensively to demonstrate they adhere to the processes and requirements laid down by the law.

Compare and contrast one group with another. For one group, process is something they have never really needed to think about in too much detail. For another group, process IS life, it is their very raison d'être.

It is no wonder therefore that when these two groups meet and 'talk process', the conversation becomes very one-sided, very confused and very unproductive. Like people talking different languages, the conversation is misunderstood, misinterpreted, and of very little value.

Unfortunately, unless managers make the effort to understand process, the CRM solution is probably doomed. Likewise, unless implementers understand sales, marketing and customer service, the solution is doomed, since process provides a common language for both sides.

What is a 'process' in CRM terms?

Process descriptions abound, and all point roughly in the same direction – so there is some consensus about what sales and marketing process actually is.

Here is a summary of some process thinking:

- Miller Heiman's Speare[4] offers process as 'a way to do something' which is 'repeatable proven and measurable' adding that processes have ' inputs, actions and outputs'. Speare identifies the sales, marketing and customer service process as 'the means of converting prospects (inputs) into Orders (Outputs). Through process, suggests Speare, 'selling is repeatable, progress can be measured, wastage reduced, throughput monitored and automation tools applied'. All this from a very achievable management technique – yet sales and marketing have predominately ignored process thinking for a long time.
- PA's Mike Marshall[5] suggests that, especially in sales and customer service, process definition must include the detail of behaviour as well as the process. From this, suggests Marshall, managers can develop 'competency frameworks' to help ensure that their team are able to implement the defined processes within certain behavioural constraints. So the job is not only done correctly, but also with the appropriate attitude. Taking

[4]Nick Speare, MD Miller Heiman Europe / Africa
[5]Mike Marshall, senior management consultant with PA Consulting

one aspect of CRM as an example, Marshall's thinking echoes the best and worst of 'typical' sales management coaching practice. How often do managers coach behaviour without specifying the detailed process associated with the behaviour? For example, coaching sales people in qualification or closing techniques is of limited benefit without providing the employee with precise details associated with the administration of the qualification process or how to book the order.

■ Brown[6] of Sales Pathways adds to the definition of process by suggesting that the modern manager should be a 'process professional' – somebody 'accountable for a result, not just a given task. His organisation also believes that 'competitive advantage will come from the ability to deliver strategy through differentiated sales process'. By having a well-developed sense of process, Brown argues that organisations are in a better position to understand what they are doing well or not so well, and make changes accordingly by suggesting that 'If you don't know what you do – how can adjustments be made?'

These examples show there is nothing magical or difficult in process thinking.

It is the 'monitor and achieve advantage' that proves the success of the process and the 'process professional' as described by Brown (above). Remember however, that in terms of CRM systems, process is not done in isolation. The total business process must include any processes that add value through integration with customers and suppliers, and processes that set the whole organisation in the context of market performance, competitors etc.

Why it is necessary to define and document process to implement a CRM solution

In the context of CRM systems, process definition is essential for the following reasons:

(a) To help monitor progress towards the vision, to help it become a reality
(b) To monitor the return on investment (ROI)
(c) To support the selection and implementation phases, including the production of training material
(d) To assist in managing and communicating further change

---

[6] Andrew Brown, Director of sales process consultancy Sales Pathways

There follows a brief consideration of each reason to undertake process definition as a pre-requisite to CRM

(a) To help monitor progress towards the vision, to help it become a reality
CRM, without vision, is little more than the application of some software tools to solve some specific operational problems. In some cases, this may be enough, and the additional operational efficiency deemed sufficient to justify the investment. However, CRM *without vision* is unlikely to provide the kind of sustainable competitive advantage that should be a major feature of these projects, neither will it satisfy the cultural change aspects of CRM.

Writing down and communicating the vision through the process definition helps to ensure its realisation. This is because managers can look at a process or group of processes and see two things. Firstly, the operational aspects of the process and how well (or otherwise), the organisation is achieving its new operational aims. Secondly, how well each aspect of the new process is playing its part in moving the organisation towards the cultural vision.

(b) To monitor the return on investment (ROI)
ROI from CRM comes from two sources. Firstly, from an improvement in the efficiency and effectiveness of the work associated with sales, marketing, and customer service. Secondly, by providing additional and sustainable competitive advantage.

With a detailed process definition, managers can clearly see where payback and advantage should come from. Without such a reference, the link between CRM solution, business process, and ROI becomes rapidly blurred, and is soon lost.

(c) To support the selection and implementation phases, including the production of training material
In practice, the only approach that avoids selecting the incorrect solution – typically one that is over- or under- specified – is the process-definition approach. With a good process definition, managers can approach CRM vendors with clear descriptions of what the solution must achieve.

Managers then score each potential solution against the process definitions. In this way, the 'dazzlement factor' added by vendors showing off their software is less likely to cloud the managers' judgement. Managers are more likely to focus on the business needs and less on investing in features that, although dazzling, do not address the core problems of the organisation.

Additionally, the process definitions carry forward to the training phase of the implementation. During the training phase, the aim is to bring together business process, CRM vision, and CRM solution. A prerequisite to this being well-defined processes.

(d) *To assist in managing and communicating change*
Simply put, 'change' means moving from one position or way of doing things to a different position or way of doing things. What is important in the CRM project is that the different positions are readily identifiable to:

a)   enable managers to change and manage the cultural aspects of CRM and
b)   as part of this management process, communicate what the change means

In particular, it is difficult to communicate that there is a change of process, if the output remains unchanged. Those involved in the process need to clearly see the 'before' and 'after' positions. Good process documentation achieves this clarity, making it easier for others to understand the change, and thereby manage the change process more effectively.

In addition, if the process change turns out to be a mistake or requires modification, it is usually possible to use the process definitions to roll back the relevant part(s) of the process change to the original position.

So in summary, process definitions and their associated scenarios provide material for monitoring the progress towards the CRM vision, for working with CRM vendors for cultural change and indeed virtually every stage of the project process.

Dealing with process improvements

Ground rules
There is little point in putting in a new system which simply systemises existing bad processes. Rather, the challenge is to determine which processes must be changed, and how much change it is sensible to introduce at one time. So, in turn, this requires a consideration of priority.

Here are some general rules regarding improvements to the process relative to implementing CRM:

1.   Don't give with one hand, and take away with the other
2.   Do ensure the basic minimum will be in place to enable the organisation to continue operating

3. Do be clear about, and communicate, the 'road-map' for system/process improvements
4. Do remember that success comes from implementing the strategy – not solving a series of problems actually created by putting in a new computer system

1. Don't give with one hand, and immediately take away with the other

The growth of high quality, feature-rich CRM software provides CRM project managers with a wealth of new functions. On the one hand, this is good, since the expectation that users have grows all the time. In addition, the ever-increasing competition that faces many firms often requires complex CRM strategies (and therefore complex CRM solutions) to address.

However, there is a danger that what was once a simple task may become a complex and unwieldy process. Understandably, users feel frustrated as they move 'one step forward and two steps back'. Although given more, it seems they have less.

A typical example is in requirements such as 'contact management'. With a simple contact manager, users create and store database records, maintain a diary, and quickly and simply interface to other applications, such as word processors and email systems. A feature-rich CRM solution should provide the same functionality (and, of course, much more). The problem comes when the bigger CRM solution appears too unwieldy to manage these simple tasks as quickly and efficiently as did the simple contact manager. Users say, 'we have a CRM strategy, and a corporate solution and a "vision". That is fine – but why does it take me 10 minutes to do something that previously took 1 minute?'

Careful planning, careful system selection and well-planned implementation can guard against this. If users can *quickly* replicate their day-to-day tasks, in a new system, they soon start to exploit the system. That means a quicker return on investment, and a faster route to making the vision of CRM a reality.

2. Do ensure the basic minimum will be in place, to enable the organisation to continue operating

With the prospect of the new and visionary, there is a temptation to forget that users require a minimum set of processes and functions to operate. The early analysis (assuming the use of the process-mapping method) identifies which these so-called 'non-stop' processes are. No interruption is permitted to these processes. Accordingly, these require a different set of procedures for implementation than do other less critical processes.

3. Do be clear about, and communicate, the 'road-map' for system / process improvements

The CRM implementation is best done on a roll-out basis, with the early project work identifying the priority for rolling out different aspects of the CRM solution. Inevitably, this means that some users are going to be disappointed with the prioritisation.

In this context, it makes sense to make explicit the long-term 'road-map' for the system roll out.

Publicising a road map provides other benefits too. If managers know which processes are 'in scope' and which processes are 'out of scope' they can plan accordingly. It can make a significant difference to ancillary / ad-hoc investments by mangers, if they are aware of what will be the complete future of the CRM strategy. Central to this theme is the importance of setting user expectations correctly.

As a guideline, remember it is always safer to promise less and deliver more – than fail to meet user expectations!

4. Do remember that success comes from implementing the strategy – not solving a series of problems actually created by putting in a new computer system

Implementing any new computer system is fraught with operational problems. The CRM solution is no different, and virtually all implementations suffer from a few bugs, operational difficulties, and related issues. Sometimes these difficulties are actually enough to bring the implementation to a grinding halt, pending a technical and/or process resolution.

Frequently, a lot of effort has to go into finding solutions to these operational / bug-related problems. Understandably, once a solution is found and work can continue there can be a sigh of relief. However, the problem is that in fixing a problem, the team may have moved away from the vision. Everyone quietly gets back to work – but the organisation is no nearer achieving its vision.

Only by ensuring that problems are fixed in the context of achieving the vision can the organisation progress.

The relationship between process improvement, strategic gain, and solution flexibility

CRM projects are notorious for high failure rates – especially in multinational projects. In CRM projects one of the biggest dangers is that huge investments are made – and there is very little real strategic change to the way the business operates. Vast sums are wasted, reputations ruined, and the organisation incurs massive 'opportunity costs'.

In the context of CRM 'failure', this means *failure to implement the vision*. Representing the vision are numerous 'process improvements'.

To understand the often 'broken' link between software feature and CRM vision it is important to understand the specific nature of one aspect of most CRM systems. Such systems are feature-rich, and particularly 'configurable'. They are generally far more configurable and flexible than ERP solutions. On the one hand, this is good. On the other hand, it can be extremely dangerous.

The problem is the pressure to get something working – *irrespective of the fit with the vision*. Success is then measured by the fact that something that 'didn't work', now 'does work' – irrespective of the benefit of the change, to the overall strategy and movement towards the vision.

This is a peculiarity of CRM solutions. Because CRM can be implemented piecemeal, it is. And in doing so, CRM attracts piecemeal changes that may be counter visionary.

Summary – process thinking

Process will be one of the main topics to challenge sales, marketing, and customer-service managers for at least the next decade or so. Process definitions enable ever smaller customer segments and ever more sophisticated routes to market, and managers must therefore remember the importance of understanding the business processes used throughout the CRM value chain. That is, charisma, gut reaction, street-wise leadership will still be important, but process expertise becomes *essential*.

In addition, the importance of 'process' will extend to process integration **between** organisations, and in managing the processes associated with e-commerce.

Furthermore, all processes – be they internal or external – will be required to take account of the impact of the wider market on the organisation, as gathered through the customer-centric CRM solution.

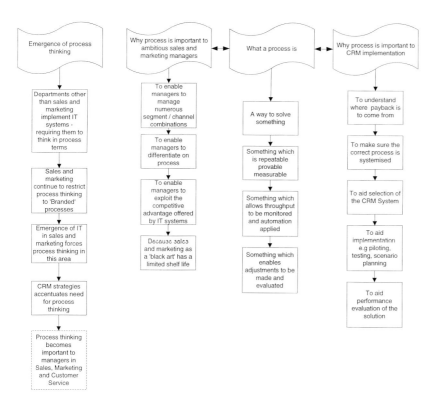

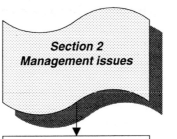

**Section 2
Management issues**

'Process' in sales and marketing
The importance of process in CRM, defining process, and dealing with process improvements

Impact of CRM on managers
How CRM changes the management role, preparing the management team, and avoiding 'opt-out' by managers

This section

Getting 'buy in'
The role of the CEO in getting buy in, understanding user needs, and calculating and presenting ROI (return on investment)

Introduction and background observations

This section considers the impact of CRM projects on 'middle-level' managers. But why is it necessary to single out one particular group of users for such an impact analysis? The answer to this is quite simple. Experience shows that, in numerous cases, the success of the CRM project is largely dependent on these 'middle-level' managers. Therefore ignoring the impact on this group is extremely risky.

"Front Office Systems[7] – an environment, not just a project". So says Dave Hanaman[8] who goes on to say "there are a lot of things to be concerned about, but too many companies (managers) focus just on the implementation. After the implementation, they find themselves in a CRM environment they are unprepared for".

Why are managers unprepared? Simply, because they fail to understand the importance of doing even basic impact analysis before embarking on their CRM project. Before such a project, managers should appreciate the likely impact on their organisation. In addition, the wise manager should consider also the impact on his or her career! Sadly, at the first 'early adopter' peak of CRM projects *c*1995, only 27% of senior managers achieved the returns they anticipated on their investment.[9] Evidence that, at that time, CRM caused severe damage to both corporate profits, and managers' careers.

There are two issues to understand. But first we need to consider what managers currently do and how their roles might change – post-CRM.

What managers actually do

Without adequate process / system combinations, most managers spend about 80% of their time trying to find out what is going on. Sales managers spend time finding out "what marketing are doing". Marketing managers spend time finding out "what sales think marketing are up to". Everyone spends time trying to work out what is really happening along the distribution channel. What spare time remains (for finding out rather than doing) goes into understanding the customer-service operation…or finding out about the customer or competitors… or finding out what else is not known about.

---

[7] FOS , Front Office Systems, another (older) term for CRM, see tables in earlier section
[8] Dave Hanaman, EVP of a US-based SFA support and training company, writing in 1998 for DCIs SFA Plus Weekly e-mail newsletter
[9] Hewson Consulting Report for Softworld in Sales and Marketing, 1996

Essentially, there is nothing wrong in this. Finding things out is an essential part of the managers' job. The problem is the proportion of time spent finding out – 80% is typical. In theory, this leaves 20% 'doing' time to address the issues found. Of course, this 20% is also required to motivate the team, recruit, plan, and perhaps help sell something, or market something, or provide customer service. Given that the CRM solution ***should tell managers what is happening***, one would expect managers would be pleased to change the time balance, i.e. between finding out and doing. After all, the CRM solution promises to do the 'finding out', thus freeing up time for managers to manage.

The problem is few managers are ready for the impact of such a change to their roles. To date, they have spent a large amount of their careers finding things out. They consider a fact found to be success. Give facts to them on a plate, and their management lives have less meaning. If you go on to make facts widely available you a) remove the knowledge power-base that some managers spend years developing and, b) prohibit managers from massaging the facts.

CRM solutions change the whole basis of work and role of managers, providing as they do the information needed to manage. Managers now must spend 20% of their time assessing the facts. Correspondingly, they must spend 80% of their time *doing something about the facts given to them*. It is no surprise, therefore, that the impact on managers is a 'fact attack'. Many find it extremely difficult to manage their time, in a world where the basis for their existence has changed:

- From concentrating on establishing what is going on to doing something about it
- From information gathering to information interpretation
- From being reactive to being proactive

So what is the impact of CRM on some individual managers? Sadly, it makes the weak manager frightened and scared, and sends him/her running for cover. It is no wonder some managers attempt to 'sabotage' these projects. Many deride such projects from the outset, hoping their poor performance can remain undiscovered. These managers are quite happy with their heads buried in the sand. *After all, with their heads in the sand they cannot see the sky falling in, so they assume it probably isn't.*

On the positive side, empirical evidence suggests that a new breed of manager is entering sales and marketing management. This new breed of manager realises that today, sales and marketing is less of a black art and requires more analytical skills now than it ever did, especially as we move towards the one-to-one marketing environment as the norm rather than the exception. So, the traditional route to senior sales management, through the 'quarterly sales leader board' (with 10 out of

10 for charisma) is not necessarily the route for future sales and marketing directors.

In the future, sales directors will achieve their position because they can manage customer relationships on a *'holistic life-time value basis'*. They will be able to do this because they understand the information delivered to them by the CRM solutions they implement. Superior Sales, Marketing, and Customer service directors will be those who have mastered CRM solutions, and are as happy with IT as they are in their traditional disciplines.

A conference footnote

As a footnote to the discussion on impact on managers, it is worth considering a recent conference on the 'changing role of the sales manager'. The Sales Consultancy[10] dedicated their client conference to the topic 'the death of the sales manager'. The conference proposition was that, with the advent of new technology, selling would no longer be 'a black art', and sales managers could safely be replaced with systems.

A lively conference agreed that whatever the sales manager is, she or he is not dead. The concern being, however, that managers' work in the future will be far more *transparent* to the rest of the organisation, making the manager concentrate on *using* information readily available, rather than finding things out on an ad-hoc basis. The conference went on to agree that, at present, measurement of performance in both sales and marketing is generally quite crude. *'Usually only simple measures are in use, such as total sales value or closing ratios'*. The conference agreed that, with the introduction of CRM, the measures of productivity become transparent to the whole organisation and increasingly sophisticated. **Therefore, transparency will change the role dramatically**.

What to do in preparation for the impact on managers of the CRM solution

Firstly, remember what Hanaman (above) and others say – these projects are not about technology. They are about people first and technology second. "This is a battle for hearts and minds" says Juer[11]. "Make sure you have top management support" says Golberg[12].

People issues are resolved early on in the successful CRM project. You do not resolve people issues by hiding behind the future, and pretending that things won't change, for they will. The project sponsors'

---

[10] A UK (Chesham)-based sales development organisation
[11] Mike Juer, veteran UK SFA practitioner
[12] Barton Golberg, President and founder of Information Systems Marketing, inc

job is to tell people right from the outset that their world is about to change. They must explain the 20% to 80% switch from finding out to doing. Give plenty of warning and tell managers 'yes, things are going to be different' and that as managers their job is to prepare for a different way of life.

Some practical preparations:

- When settled on a CRM vendor, ask if your managers can talk with some of the managers at the vendor's other clients. Managers must make an effort to understand the scope and scale of the changes that are to follow; sharing experiences in this way is of enormous benefit.
- Direct managers to the various networking and Internet resources dealing with this topic.[13].
- Direct managers to make a list of how their approach and job might change, if they have the information they need, when they need it

Be careful, however, not to over-sell the solution. Do not imply the system can do more than it will, or produce more information sooner. Doing this will, simply, lead to a different set of problems. At this stage, the aim is to get managers to change their mind-set. Managers need to appreciate that CRM solutions facilitate cultural change but, in themselves, are not cultural change.

Beware of management casualties and opt-outs

Managers who are not ready to receive facts and reports from a new system have a tendency to put the new information to one side immediately on receiving it. These managers continue to operate as before. Whilst the 7-figure investment on CRM steadily provides information, the 5- or even 6-figure managers carry on searching elsewhere for information. To avoid these and similar problems there must be an emphasis on preparation.

If there are to be casualties, find out quickly. Role-playing and discussion and involvement before the system goes live provides excellent opportunities for senior management to identify which managers are going to struggle in the new environment.

The worst a senior manager can do is to forgo the opportunity to gather these early warning signs, and suffer management acceptance problems in the ranks on the day of implementation.

---

[13]Networking / support groups include Sistrum in Euroupe, see www.hewson.co.uk or the web-based service from DCI see www.sfaplus.dci.com

Summary, the impact on managers

Managers must acknowledge that new process / system combinations change the basis of work. For many managers, this change implies an eroding of their knowledge-based power. It implies making managers more accountable for how output is achieved, and less able to claim 'lack of knowledge' as a defence to poor performance.

On the other hand, good CRM solutions provide many opportunities to enable good managers to manage even more effectively, and the CRM solution should be introduced within this context of more effective performance, overall.

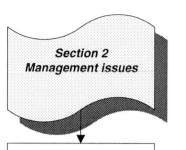

**Section 2
Management issues**

'Process' in sales and marketing
The importance of process in CRM, defining process, and dealing with process improvements

Impact of CRM on managers
How CRM changes the management role, preparing the management team, and avoiding 'opt-out' by managers

This section

Getting 'buy in'
The role of the CEO in getting buy in, understanding user needs, and calculating and presenting ROI (return on investment)

Getting initial 'buy-in' from the management team

The starting point for a successful project is to achieve the right run level of funding, plus political / emotional support at the right levels within the organisation. Generally, this means getting fellow managers to agree that scarce resources need spending on a CRM strategy, rather than on something else. Above all, it means getting the CEO sold on CRM – this is essential.

Getting all managers to agree to a CRM strategy requires crossing many organisational boundaries. At a minimum, it means achieving consensus from managers in Sales, Marketing, and Customer Service. To achieve this consensus, it requires the sponsoring manager to set the right scope for the system and understand the likely impact of his/her ideas on other managers – and, of course, for all managers to agree and share the vision.

Key buy in issues – and the role of the CEO

There are both strong operational and strategic reasons why it is essential to achieve buy-in at CEO and senior manager level. The strategic necessity is because of the visionary nature of these projects. *True* CRM changes the 'hearts and minds' of the organisation and changes the culture. Not least, it can shift the balance of power from individual 'silos' within the organisation (Sales, Marketing, and Customer service) to power *based on cross-organisational processes*. End-to-end processes, for example, such as processes associated with customer retention or the maintenance of the segmentation strategy. To achieve these visionary changes it is, naturally enough, essential to have support from the senior management team representing the end-to-end value chain.

There should be no difficulty in getting management colleagues to agree to 'a computer-based system to improve sales, marketing, and customer service'. After all, most managers understand that if they have a problem, a likely solution might be the introduction of new technology and, in any case, with a proven need, nobody is going to openly vote *against* 'improvement'.

The media, various management gurus, management consultants, and numerous trade journals weigh in with their arguments. In general, most support investment in this area, i.e. they support the investment in IT systems to increase competitive advantage in Sales, Marketing and Customer service. Again, most managers agree with these industry specialists. It is hard not to accept such logical arguments.

Therefore, facilitating change using new technology should be relatively straightforward. It should be but, as many CRM practitioners know, it is not. In reality, project managers find 'hidden agenda' items, and departmental 'turf wars' give them real difficulty in obtaining buy-in for CRM projects. It is only the foolish manager who underestimates these difficulties, and attempts to ride roughshod over his/her colleagues' concerns. All the logic in the world rarely defeats an emotionally charged, territory-defending colleague; a colleague more concerned that the proposed system is going to rock the boat and cast them into inhospitable waters, than with the imperative to achieve productivity gains.

A good starting point to diffusing buy-in issues, and getting fellow managers on board, is to get managers to agree what problem it is the system should be resolving. Although this in itself is frequently problematic, nevertheless, it is a good starting point.

So...what is the problem? – What is wrong with the 'old' vision or existing solutions that support customer relationship management?

If managers cannot agree on 'the problem' they are not likely to agree (and therefore support) 'the solution'. Of course, there is never a single problem. In addition, the definition of the problem takes a different form, depending on the perspective of the manager or workgroup involved. One group's problem is another group's opportunity. A downside to one group is an upside to another. A major difficulty to one group is only a minor irritation to another – and vice versa.

Managers do not need to agree verbatim on 'the terms of engagement' for the project. Problem definition should not be like some peace treaty between warring factions, where there is no peace until reaching agreement on every word. Managers need to accept a considerable degree of apparent disparity at the problem definition stage. More importantly, managers must sign up to the vision– not just to solving a range of operational problems.

To define 'the problem' at an early stage in the project, managers require an understanding of four essential aspects:

- Who the users might be – *i.e. identify the 'system boundary'*
- What their needs are – *i.e. what problems or potential improvements might the solution address?*
- What impact the solution should / might have on the business process? – *i.e. where does the solution fit with vis-à-vis the business process?*
- What is the cost justification case – *i.e. where is the ROI coming from?*

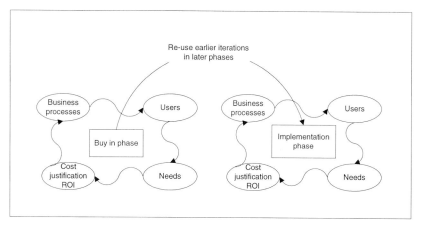

Iterating 4 key issues, as part of the buy in phase and, later, part of the implementation phase

Armed with this knowledge, managers can target their influential colleagues both inside and outside the organisation. It then becomes possible to discuss needs and associated business processes – and enlist fellow managers' support in the buy-in process.

Furthermore, the work on these key aspects feeds directly into the early stages of the implementation process. Therefore, it is possible to re-use work done at the buy-in stage in the early stages of the implementation, as the diagram above shows.

Who the users might be

The major step in securing a budget and political support is to identify clearly the 'system boundary'. At the same time, this helps reveal the range of problems the solution is to address, and bring to an operational level the opportunities for increased competitive advantage through CRM.

A system boundary simply describes the scope of the organisational boundaries the new system is likely to encompass, and who are likely to be the users of the system. The boundary helps to identify all the 'stakeholders' potentially involved in the new system and consider their problems. *At the same time, remembering it is solutions one is after – not problems* since no firm ever improved competitive advantage simply by producing a list of problems!

The system boundary of the CRM systems is generally far wider than the boundary normally encountered by an individual Sales,

Marketing, or Customer Service manager. The obvious parts of the boundary, and what it encompasses, are indeed obvious. These parts are easy to identify and, usually, less problematical.

Departments involved in CRM

Department	*Preliminary problem / solution identification and opportunity spotting*
Research and development dept	They may need a better understanding of customer needs, more quickly. Would it help having sales people feed info electronically to them, directly from the customer base?
Product managers	This group spend too long on the 'phone repeating the same information to different sales people. Perhaps a system might help form part of a central knowledge resource.
Marketing dept	Numerous needs; focusing though on a corporate database and supporting channel partners. The solution should also help automate the company database and manage campaigns, especially those directed through channel partners. Currently, campaigns take too long to set up, and there is no 'closed loop' process.
Sales dept	Numerous needs, current main issue is 'account management'. Sales are struggling with what account management means *in practice*. Systemisation may help introduce a standardised approach to key account management.
Customer service dept	Currently these have their own system, used in isolation to account managers and accounts. Integration between these solutions would be useful, and avoid duplicating data and repetitive 'phone calls from sales to customer services, explaining situations.
Accounts / finance dept	Currently these have their own systems, used in isolation to account managers – who constantly need to know credit status and delivery / invoice position. Integration between these solutions would be useful, and avoid duplicating data and repetitive 'phone calls from sales to accounts and finance, explaining situations.
IT dept	Currently maintaining numerous systems and databases – and several different versions of PC and software solutions. Standardisation of a single system and single database may reduce the overall support overhead.
Personnel dept	Responsible for productivity analysis, and are having problems gathering activity data from sales marketing and customer-service dept. In addition, personnel have requests for a new commission system, requiring better sales and sales person activity data to implement.

The difficult areas are those which are generally less obvious, yet are extremely critical and subsequently become extremely problematic. Experience shows that the inexperienced project manager assumes the boundary is limited to immediate departments, such as Sales or Marketing or Customer Service – and perhaps only sees the smallest of overlap between these departments. In reality, the overlap is normally considerable between all departments and extends outside the immediate organisation – or rather it should, in order to implement true CRM.

The table above shows some of the departments that might be included in the 'System boundary', together with some of the solutions the CRM solution may provide.

External stakeholder

External stakeholder identification	Preliminary problem / solution
Channel partners	A process that is more effective for managing sales leads given to channel partners is required, plus a solution to minimise channel conflicts. Could systems help resolve some of these issues?
Key account customers	Recent survey revealed request for greater 'transparency' in account management, and faster response to special pricing.
Sister companies in other countries	Opportunity to share leads and leverage account / prospect knowledge, across a wider geography.
Subsidiaries in xyz business	Opportunity to cross-sell and up-sell, by exchanging data on existing accounts.
Suppliers of special products	Constant request for longer notice on special delivery orders. Would improvements in forecasting help these suppliers, and therefore enable us to drive down the cost of specials?
Lead handling agency	Process for verifying duplicate database records is very tedious – could the lead handling agency use the same system for their lead management as eventually the company chooses?
Company providing data on market performance	Market performance data currently resides in spreadsheets, unconnected with segment performance. Could a new system help present actual performance data more quickly, into the context of market performance?
Credit checking agency	'Routine' credit checks take 3 days to get a response to the sales person in the field – unless there is manual intervention. Could the system help speed up this process, perhaps to a daily turnaround or a few hours?

Having considered the internal system boundary, it is then important to look outside of the immediate organisation, and assess the impact of 'external' stakeholders. See table above.

In deciding on the system boundary, remember the 'boundary' may well extend beyond the organisation. For example, for 'real' CRM the boundary should extend into the customers' system / process combinations, and possibly that of the suppliers. It may also extend to other parts of the group, such as offices in other countries or associated group of companies. Increasingly, as e-commerce comes into the equation, the extended system boundary widens still further.

In addition, many firms are moving to 'world-wide' CRM solutions, reflecting that their customers buy and require services on a global basis. These global companies increasingly expect their suppliers to understand their organisations, on a world-wide basis, i.e. to subsequently structure the CRM strategy on a global basis. Potentially, this widens the boundary yet further.

Moreover, extending the boundary to an associated company (i.e. parent / sister company) may offer benefits of cross- and up-selling. This provides the opportunity to share data and customer knowledge throughout a group, and add value accordingly.

1. Understanding users' needs
Having identified the likely users of the system – the 'system boundary' – it is time to identify how the CRM systems may affect each department, and the interaction between each department.

A useful (though admittedly dated) formula is the 'People Process Technology' formula. Each potential user-department is considered in the context of People, Process and Technology. In practice, it is necessary to consider all those within the system boundaries, i.e. all those in the internal and the external system boundary – rather than a selection as shown in the table over the page. Each potential user-group is considered, at a high level, in the context of 'people, process and technology'.

What the 'system boundary' and a consideration of 'People Process Technology' accomplish
The system boundary table provides a simple high-level view of where to find 'problems / solutions', i.e. clearly identifying the departments involved. The People Process Technology table then drills down into these problem / solution areas, identifying more detailed issues likely to impact on the organisation. This table also helps to unearth recent system expenditure, and other system plans that may overlap with the emerging CRM solution strategy.

Table showing selective drill down 'into system boundary elements', to consider people, process, and technology issues

Department	People	Business Process	Technology
Product management	Sales support specialists	Providing field sales with product information	Currently via 'phone and e-mail. Could move to centralised intranet – and possibly a secure extranet.
		Reporting to marketing	Weekly meetings going over call reports. CRM systems could automate process and provide data for meetings.
Sales	Field sales representatives	Call reporting	Various technologies in use – but no possibility of providing standard reports quickly.
		Account management	Process requires greater connectivity with accounts – for example, field-based e-mail.
		Time management	Must replace manual systems –too clumsy.
		Researching potential accounts	Via the Internet?
		Forecasting	Introduce an integrated system, to remove the dependency on sharing spreadsheets.
	Telesales	Scheduling call backs	Assisted selling over the web?
		Handling incoming calls –	CTI (Computer Telephony Integration).
		Liasing with field sales	Connect field and head office, via the dial up CRM systems.
Account / Finance	Accounts clerks	Updating sales people	Remove need for direct contact – integrate data.
		On-hold accounts	Remove need for direct contact – integrate data.
Channel partners	Channel sales representatives	Lead handling	Manage leads via web interface.
		Channel conflict management	Manage leads via web interface.
Sister companies in xyz business	Sales people	Generating new leads	Automate lead handling process – capture and auto share web leads.
Marketing data providers	Tele- researchers	Qualifying leads	Send new leads via e-mail.
		Providing data	Give qualifiers access via the web – using restricted web interface.

Gathering some idea of the current technology in use is useful for two reasons. Firstly, it helps to give an idea of the degree of challenge there might be in moving to alternative technologies. Secondly, it helps to identify recent expenditure on systems. This is useful, since managers who have recently invested heavily in a system may resent having to either undo part of their solution to accommodate a corporate wide CRM solution, or fund more investment in new systems.

Put together, these tables then help to identify the most likely areas of impact across both the internal and external organisation. More importantly, the tables then provide sufficient detail to start matching the CRM solution requirements onto a CRM process, and calculating the potential ROI (Return On Investment).

Calculating ROI – Return On Investment

Herein lies one of the major problems of getting budgetary approval for a CRM solution. Generally, firms considering an investment in CRM have only rudimentary systems. These systems provide little in the way of management data, to identify specific costs. So, most firms have problems measuring the cost of specific aspects of their end-to-end Sales, Marketing and Customer Service business process.

It is rarely possible, therefore, to categorically say that an improvement of X percentage in productivity is to bring Y financial return – the data to support such claims not being available. Managers are left with little choice but either to a) undertake cost analysis based on what little data may be available or b) take an educated guess.

The problem with a) is the requirement to collect the necessary data, to get approval for the proposed system. Without suitable systems (which of course do not exist) collecting data is a very long-winded and difficult process. Gathering satisfactory and robust data may involve analysis over a long period – and in collecting this data momentum can be lost. Often, therefore, managers must take an 'educated guess' and use their intuition.

Frameworks for ROI on CRM

Managers do, however, require a framework around which to build their own ROI calculations and assessments. The following are two such frameworks which are to be used together. The first to identify general ROI trends, the second to apply these to the CRM environment.

The first framework, represents a potential high-level view, from which it should be possible to see beneficial ROI in general terms.

The second framework uses the generic CRM process. This framework should help managers identify specific CRM process-related ROI opportunities – or at least give a pointer as to where to look.

Framework 1 – a model for CRM productivity.
  The diagram below illustrates a framework model for CRM productivity. Each element in the framework represents a key factor in the productivity equation. For maximum productivity, there must be a balance of efficiency **between** these factors. For example, it is typical that an organisation which is 'moderately efficient' in all aspects of the framework model is, overall, more efficient than an organisation excelling in just one or two areas. 'Efficiency' in terms of the elements in the model differs. For example, efficiency in *'understanding market behaviour'* is different to *'efficiency in measuring the metrics associated with CRM'*. Nevertheless, through examining strengths and weakness within and between each element, managers can begin to see clearly where CRM should provide a real return.

  In practice, the model is used in a matrix format, to present the opportunities for ROI from the interaction between each element. Each element represents one of the key factors impacting on productivity in the CRM environment:

1. Ability to understand market behaviour, relative to effectiveness of channel and segmentation strategy
  Organisations that are able to measure their channel and distribution strategy based on real market analysis are able to use their resources more

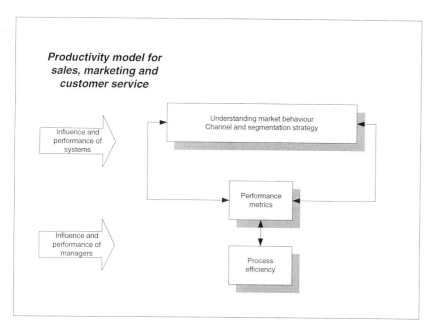

productively. These organisations base their decisions on the facts from the market – capturing and using these facts far more quickly and effectively than organisations unable to do this. The CRM solution should (assuming it includes reference to the external market) provide the necessary data to achieve productivity gains in this area.

2. How well current systems perform

An essential element in the productivity model is simply the performance of existing systems. It is worth noting that in many cases firms might raise productivity considerably simply by improving their basic systems, without recourse to a full CRM implementation. Indeed, given the elapsed time required to implement CRM, an interim strategy to improve productivity may be to look for a short-term improvement in existing systems, pending CRM to encourage cultural change.

3. Availability to measure metrics along relevant value chain / Ability to measure process efficiency

If an organisation has little knowledge of how it is performing, it is extremely difficult to make significant productivity gains. Within the framework model, *organisations that are more productive* measure their process and performance metrics efficiency relative to market performance. Also, they evaluate the impact of systems and managers. *Less productive organisations* struggle to understand what is going on. They make adjustments based on unsound data.

4. How well current systems help managers influence performance

Systems should enable managers to influence performance, as much as they enable managers to monitor performance. And how positively or how negatively managers contribute to productivity is of critical concern in respect of achieving maximum productivity. If managers can identify at an earlier stage and take the right corrective action, naturally, productivity gains should follow. **Good CRM solutions put managers in the driving seat in this respect.**

Framework 2 – a process model, used to identify specific productivity gains, leading to greater ROI.

The following generic CRM process model provides an indication of where to look for ROI – accepting that the specifics of each case will be unique. Using the generic CRM process model and notes below, managers should use the model to determine areas for productivity improvement and therefore enhanced ROI.

Framework model 2 operates in conjunction with framework model 1 (above)

Segmentation strategies

CRM provides greater granularity in planning and managing more numerous customer segments. This should lead to more cost efficiencies and productivity gains in implementing segmentation strategies.

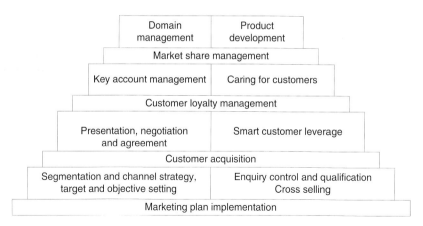

Generic CRM process model

This is because of the greater efficiency in targeting – simply getting the right information to the right prospects can save thousands on sales and marketing costs. Furthermore, with CRM, the segmentation strategy should extend to account management and thereby have a positive impact on customer retention (see below).

For example, an improvement in correctly targeting specific segments or locating the correct individual within an organisation may save x% on the variable cost of a campaign. Of course, calculating 'x' is the challenge but, based on an understanding of existing systems, managers should be able to make an educated guess as to its value.

Channel management

Channel management costs include the cost of the margin surrendered to the channel in return for their efforts and the direct costs of managing the channel.

The most significant channel-related ROI for most organisations comes from using CRM simply to understand the cost of selling through the channel – and then doing something about reducing it. At a high level, managers might assume an ever-increasing percentage of ROI, *proportional to the current lack of knowledge about channel costs*, i.e. the less that is currently known, the greater the likelihood of making productivity gains. It is possible, therefore, to take the total known costs and apply some sensible savings – say 5%-25%.

Not least, specific and significant ROI comes from reducing communication costs (through e-CRM strategies) and managing channel conflict more effectively and productively.

Targeting and objective setting

CRM provides the data that help managers to more accurately set targets and objectives. Although the value of this is difficult to quantify, most organisations can get a return on investment in CRM through being able to more accurately set their targets and objectives – i.e. set them relative to more accurate data taken from the CRM solution.

In addition, CRM provides superior monitoring of targets and objectives, leading to swifter action to put the organisation back on course if things look like going wrong. Again, this may be difficult to quantify, but in practice provides a valuable return.

Enquiry control

For some organisations, generating and handling high-volume enquiries can be a time-consuming and expensive business. Therefore, managers should be able to do straightforward calculations to show productivity gains from the CRM solution. For example, saving on labour costs is typical since CRM automates much of both the enquiry generation and processing processes – and more importantly helps to improve closing ratios.

In addition, the enquiry-control process should become more effective, with the added process granularity provided by the CRM solution. This leads to a greater understanding of the relationship between marketing effort and sales reward.

Cross-selling and up-selling

CRM should provide the data to help drive both cross-selling and up-selling strategies. Whether the sales team exploits this data and associated processes is, of course, a change-management issue.

Nevertheless, potentially the CRM solution offers a good return in this area – but again, this return is extremely difficult to calculate and generally dependent on winning the 'battle for hearts and minds'.

A rough calculation might suggest that say if x accounts have cross / up-selling potential, and the new CRM strategy enables the firm to realise the potential in just half of these accounts, that is probably still a significant contribution to the ROI.

Presentation, negotiation, closing

The benefits of CRM at the point of sale revolve around making the right data and information available to the sales person, and putting the sales person in the right place at the right time. Whether the sales person exploits the data, and thereby achieves a respectable ROI, is a different issue.

Nevertheless, it is fair to credit the CRM solution with the *ability* to make sure the sales person gets in front of the right people at the right time, and presents the right products or services. Again, theoretically, this should improve ROI.

Specific improvements come through the ability of the CRM solution to provide superior contact and time management. Coupling this with greater segmentation granularity means that, once in front of the prospect, the sales presentation should be more relevant than even before – and the sales person rewarded with more orders accordingly (all things being equal of course...).

However, all ROI so closely associated with the performance of the individual is notoriously difficult to calculate, and requires careful treatment in the investment case.

For hard data, look to use CRM to:

- Improve call frequency and timing to maximize the use of field resources (consider calculating what just a 5% improvement in field productivity would provide)
- Calculate the impact of various improvements on closing ratios
- Calculate the impact of various improvements on qualification efficiency

Smart customer leverage

Remembering that 'Smart Customer Leverage' is about making the most of a customer as an asset, CRM should score highly for ROI in this area.

For example, strategies include leveraging existing customers within an industry sector to generate more business within the sector, and leveraging within the group of companies to which the customer belongs.

However, as with all sales and marketing activity at the point of sale, ROI on customer leverage activity is a 'leap of faith' when it comes to ROI on CRM.

The ROI is available, but requires careful extraction – especially since it requires cross-departmental co-ordination through Sales, Marketing, and Customer service. Anyone looking for 'hard benefits' should steer clear of leverage for an answer; those looking for 'soft' benefits will find plenty in this area.

Key account management

Many firms are now waking up to the reality that 'Key Account Management' equates to 'Customer Retention'. Therefore, look in this area for some of the hard benefits that CRM brings to customer-retention strategies.

Although well-worn as a theory, it is therefore worth calculating the cost of finding new accounts vs the cost of customer retention. Impressive ROI figures relate to reducing customer defection by even a few percentage points.

Therefore, the ROI case for the CRM solution can come from stemming customer defections. This is achieved by implementing superior Key Account Management using the CRM solution. For hard data, look to the impact of x% customer retention, vs the cost of acquiring a new account.

Caring for customers

'Caring for customers' is the operational aspect of the strategic 'Key Account Management' activity and, in general, ROI related to customer care is usually very calculable, and provides long-term savings. In this area, therefore, look for ROI from hard benefits associated with savings at every 'customer-touch' point.

For example, mapping the activity directly related to customer care often reveals process inefficiencies, such as those relating to data management and carrying out simple administrative routines.

CRM reduces numerous repetitive data entry and retrieval tasks, and speeds up the delivery of services given direct to the customer. Most firms have process inefficiencies in these areas, and can usually find plenty of reasons here to finance an investment.

Domain management

'Domain management' refers to the business of managing the processes relating to CRM. ROI from the CRM solution in this area comes from managers having a far better understanding of what the business is actually doing.

For example, management reports from the CRM solution should give a better indication of where resources are being used, and how effective each process is.

ROI and management intuition – the 'leap of faith' approach

'CRM? – Still partly a leap of faith', so says veteran CRM market watcher Nick Hewson. Hewson goes on to say that 'whatever ROI number managers arrive at, it is the "vision" that eventually tips the balance in green lighting these projects'.

Hewson's suggestion is that in the long run, mainly due to changes in the business environment, managers have little option but to 'do' CRM – as integrated solutions. That organisations have little option on CRM is widely acknowledged – but not sufficient argument for failing to consider where the return is to come from. So, in summary, a 'gut reaction' is that the ROI case should be based on 50% hard facts and 50% intuition. Beyond this, either way, the case is likely to be so overwhelmingly in favour of or overwhelmingly against investment that the final decision will take little effort.

There is a certain paradox in deciding on the scope of the CRM solution. By definition, the scope of the system should encompass 'every aspect of Sales, Marketing and Customer Service'. The paradox is that the scope cannot be so wide at the outset, since few organisations can accommodate so much change.

In any case, organisations rarely sign up to across-the-board change. They generally like to address themselves to very specific issues. Therefore, we see the scoping exercise as being a reflection of what senior management feels a need to prioritise, as much as what the organisation really requires.

Managers are determining what is broken, and the priority and effort that should go into fixing what is broken. In addition, there will be some career-making (or -breaking) aspect to the decision-making process – i.e. the political angle.

In practical terms, the simplest approach when considering priorities and phases is to create a table showing what is considered to be top priority and therefore important for the short term, what is for the mid term, and what is for the long term. Then, at least, managers will have something to work on. Typically, this leaves the final scoping exercise as a decision for the whole management team.

An added complexity of the CRM project, however, concerns dealing with dependencies relating to data and integration. For example, a top priority might be to provide a company-wide, single database of customers and prospects. Which may be dependent on integrating numerous databases from equally numerous systems. Which is dependent on gathering the data in the first place.

In short, prioritisation is essential but requires an understanding of all the project dependencies, of which in the CRM project there are many – plus the ability to look across the whole organisation.

Benefit dependency network

A useful approach in the CRM implementation is to adapt the Cranfield 'Benefits Dependency Network' technique, to drive the scoping exercise. This technique simply requires managers to define the pathway to a benefit and ensure that everything is in place to achieve the benefit. Since CRM works across the organisation, this technique serves as a useful check list to ensure that anticipated benefits are in fact going to accrue, using the proposed roll-out sequence (i.e. all the necessary interconnections will be in place).

Proving the ROI (Return On Investment) case

In the CRM project, facing the manager are more than likely to be decisions unsupported by data. Decisions requiring all the experience and intuition of the business manager – rather than the analytical skills of the management accountant. In the real world, therefore, we find it is easy to make a claim about a return. However, *substantiating* that claim to a sceptical management team – deciding between competing investment options – may not be so easy.

Here are a few examples, taken from real projects, where managers had difficulty justifying their claims. The examples do not necessarily mean those making a proposal, or those considering the manager's proposals are 'wrong' or 'right' in their line of thinking or questioning. They simply show the thoroughness required when presenting a benefit analysis, and that managers do not always think or agree with 'the obvious'.

- **Using the CRM system, sales people will save time**
  No one disputes the time saving – but what precisely will they do with the time they save? As a result of this, will they sell more per person, or do we need fewer sales people? If they will sell more per person, how much more? If we need fewer people, how many fewer? Or, will our investment just give sales people an easier time, in exchange for no increase in productivity? If there is to be an increase in productivity, how is it to be measured? If there are to be fewer people, how will the project team manage the process of reducing the size of the sales team?

- **The CRM systems will help us to know more about our customers**
  Good, it would be good to know more about the customer base, but armed with that knowledge what will we do? How will we use the knowledge to either increase sales or reduce costs? What don't we know that we think we ought to know? Also, what plans are there to retrain the sales and marketing team to take advantage of this new-found knowledge? And where is the data coming from – what have the IT dept said about providing customer sales data, whilst the new data warehouse and ERP goes live over the next 2 years?

- **We can use the laptops for presenting our services, as well as managing the CRM solution**
  So how much effort is to go into preparing presentations and getting these from marketing to sales? Does this mean marketing are going to be knee-deep in presentation software for weeks on end? And, how precisely will we get a return on this? What research has been done to prove that customers will buy more? With the new system will the customer pay a higher price or defect from the competition simply because the sales

people use a PC instead of an old-fashioned presenter? Where is the research to prove these claims – or are they just hunches and gut reaction?

Although in these examples the line of questioning may appear cynical, the questions raised are fair. After all, the empirical evidence to date is that CRM systems do not, on their own, produce a good return. To get a good return requires a well-thought-out plan, good implementation, and ongoing project management.

Introducing 'iteration'

Before progressing it is necessary to pause and consider the place of 'iteration' in the CRM project process.

Iteration is a key concept in the implementation of any system-based solution – be it the implementation of a single all-encompassing system or many integrated solutions. Simply put, iteration refers to going over the same ground on several occasions – and (hopefully) adding to the project in a beneficial way, through each iteration.

Of course, in an ideal world, there would be no need for iteration. Managers and technologists would get everything right, first time. CRM is not this ideal world. Not least, what drives the need to iterate in this environment is its dynamic nature. Sales, Marketing and Customer service rarely stands still from one quarter to the next. Without several iterations, the time lag between inception and implementation may result in missing many important changes in the environment that should be reflected in the solution.

The place of iteration in the buy-in stage

From a practical perspective, managers need to balance the amount of work done at the buy-in stage with the work required to plan and implement the solution. To this end, the concept of iteration is extremely useful. Under cover of iteration, managers can present the first iteration of their thinking on several issues, safe in the knowledge that as the project progresses there can be other more detailed iterations.

Therefore, without going into too much detail – or using up too many resources – managers can undertake 'first-cut' analysis, before getting all-round approval.

The CRM project touches many parts of the organisation, and can have an impact on innumerable business processes. The sponsoring manager therefore needs to know just who in the organization is likely to be involved, and in what capacity relative to the implementation of the CRM solution. This knowledge is required to help identify issues and enlist support.

Presenting the CRM project – as a 'day in the life of' scenario

This section considers a method to present the benefits of the proposed investment. The method assumes that the presentation audience have an idea of the Sales, Marketing and Customer service processes – but are not familiar with the detail – a realistic scenario.

The following is an outline for a 'day in the life of' presentation. The objective of the presentation being to get approval to spend more time (and more importantly money), on investigating the implementation of a CRM solution, i.e. to get the CRM project underway.

The presentation is in 3 sections:

1. An overview of why there is a need for a new CRM strategy
2. Where the return on investment is to come from
3. A 'day in the life of' some of the users of the new system supporting the strategy

1.   Why there is a need for a new CRM vision and associated CRM solution

This section should include the factors gathered from the earlier investigative work, presented from the perspective of four main groups – plus of course an endorsement of the vision from the CEO.

a)   The management / senior management team – i.e. the strategic 'vision' view
b)   The main users of the system – i.e. the operational view
c)   Channel partners- i.e. distributors and also other partners such as suppliers
d)   Competitors – i.e. a consideration of the likely response by competitors

The presentation needs to frame the analysis of the CRM process, in the context of each of a) to d) above. The presentation should illustrate in broad terms why the investment will improve the business from the perspective of each group.

Considering the likely response of competitors is especially important concerning any 'virtual' part of the strategy. Internet strategies (as opposed to extranet[14] strategies that are more controllable) are by their nature very transparent to the competition, as are competitive responses.

---

[14] 'Extranet' is the term given where a firm makes information available on a restricted web site. For example, only available via a password to customers or authorised users.

Assuming the completion of each stage, i.e. problem / solution generation, and CRM process analysis, this should be a relatively straightforward task.

2. Where the ROI is to come from?

Where is the return on investment going to come from, and in what form? For example, will the ROI come from increased sales, reduced costs or increased customer loyalty? Will it come from increased sales of higher margin business or from reducing low margin, high-risk business?

In addition, what data is available against which the ROI can be measured – and what data is not available at present? It is necessary to present both available data and show what is not currently available, so as to illustrate in advance if there is likely to be any ambiguity about presenting the business case.

Presenting ROI for CRM systems is in stark contrast to justifying investment in other systems such as manufacturing or distribution systems. In these projects, there is detailed financial data more readily available. In addition, manufacturing and distribution systems clearly show 'cause and effect' – 'If we do this...that will happen'. In CRM systems the outcome is not nearly so clear. For example, there is no *guarantee* that improving customer service will necessarily improve customer retention. It should, but there are many other factors to take into account.

In CRM presentations, managers must frequently rely on instinct more than proven cause and effect. Project sponsors must be ready to answer those awkward questions designed to strike at the heart of an argument based on instinct and gut reaction.

In practice, the best way to present the potential return is to give an effective 'day in the life of' presentation, outlined below.

3. A 'day in the life of' ... some of the users of the proposed solution

The 'day in the life of' presentation is an opportunity to display the project team's 'vision for the future'. In doing so, the team compares the current situation with how things might be following the implementation of the CRM solution. Most importantly, the vision shows how the investment solves real problems, generates a financial return, and actually addresses the strategic needs of the organisation.

Because the project crosses so many organisational boundaries, all the stakeholders need to be in unison and agree to the investment. Therefore the aim of the 'day in the life of' presentation is to get the management team as a whole to agree that the risk is:

a) Worth taking
b) A risk to be shared between all the 'stakeholders'

Otherwise, the new CRM systems and associated processes will only be as good as the weakest link in the chain.

The 'day in the life of' presentation would for example show:

- The new process for establishing, running, and monitoring a marketing campaign – compared to the old process
- The new process for responding to a customer-service request, compared to the old process
- The reports managers will have to work within the new, as opposed to the old, environment
- The benefits to the customer – on a day-to-day basis, as a result of the changes towards a CRM-centric environment

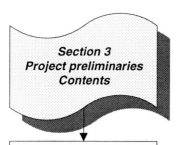

**Section 3
Project preliminaries
Contents**

Establishing the project team
Creating a balanced CRM team, and the composition of the team

Estimating CRM project costs
Typical project costs, and the likely cost areas: hardware, software and services, costs which are difficult to determine

Project risk - a high level view
Risks at the pre-launch and implementation stages

Section 3
Project preliminaries

This section

Establishing the project team
Creating a balanced CRM team, and the composition of the team

Estimating CRM project costs
Typical project costs, and the likely cost areas: hardware, software and services, costs which are difficult to determine

Project risk - a high level view
Risks at the pre-launch and implementation stages

Introduction

The size and scope of the project will determine the actual number in the project team. However all projects, practically irrespective of size, need certain roles to be filled. This section considers these roles and offers managers some working guidelines on how to identify the roles, and obtain an understanding of the likely time commitment **per role.**

A major determinant of the project team is the general context in which the team is to operate, i.e. the cross-organisational nature of the CRM project; the fact that it involves IT and non-IT professionals. That CRM projects require both visionaries and practical 'hands on' people, gives some idea of the need to think carefully about the project team.

In addition, the project will most likely involve managing several external relationships. These will include suppliers to the CRM project (vendor(s), trainers, and consultants) and ancillary providers such as database providers, lead-handling agencies, and many other external supporting organisations.

Project team 'balance'

In this context, 'balance', means ensuring that the CRM does not become *only* a marketing system, or *only* a sales system, or *only* an e-commerce system, or *only* a customer-care system. That is, without the correct balance in the project, the CRM strategy ends up as a *tactical* solution rather than an as integrated sales, marketing, customer service/e-commerce system.

Having the wrong balance in the team may result in inadvertently removing the "vision" from a CRM project, making the 'CRM project' a simple operational exercise. It becomes one of implementing some software tools to solve an operational issue. This happens, for example, when one group of managers – biased to their departmental needs – dominates the project, neglecting to think sufficiently **across** the organisation. Their ideas and possibly their personal vision (in contrast to the corporate vision) dominates the project. In part, the way to avoid this is to ensure a 'well-balanced' project team, and thereby avoid over-dominance by one group of managers.

Whilst lack of balance can happen in any project, it is more prone in CRM, because of the cross-functional nature of the project.

It is against the following background that the project team needs forming:

- Cross-departmental use of CRM
- The need to turn a vision into a reality
- The need to maintain a balance
- The need to do better things

Size and composition of the project team

To cover the wide range of projects, it is only sensible to provide guidelines. Subsequently, managers can apply the guidelines to their own situation. What is important in providing the guidelines is to clearly identify both the role, and provide some indication of the time investment associated with the role.

Composition of the project team

The CRM project operates at two levels, strategic and operational. This requires both 'movers and shakers' to be in the team, representing the vision of the CEO and senior management team and 'doers'.

Specifically, the project team requires:

- **Movers and shakers from each user department associated with the project.** *Not necessarily in a full-time capacity, but to be aware of what is going on, and in a position to smooth the path for the operational people, and make refereeing decisions on a regular basis. Be clear, these movers and shakers are not just figureheads of the project. They have to participate at crucial times, by making these refereeing decisions. They need to understand how to create sensible process flows across organisational boundaries, where none currently exist.*
- **Senior IT representative.** *A project team member representing the IT director is an absolute must. The IT department have to have a clear line into the project, not least because of the impact of the implementation on other IT projects, and vice versa. Do not accept a 'low-level' IT contact. It is important to represent CRM at the highest IT level. The CRM solution will require data from other systems within the organisation – and the IT representative on the team is likely to be tasked to get that data.*
- **Operational representatives.** *Every potential user department needs representing from an operational perspective. These operational representatives need to understand the business process within their 'silo' and how the processes fit together to form end-to-end business processes. This is a job for an enthusiast who will champion the CRM project, and one who already has a good*

understanding of what the organisation does and why it operates in the way it does. Not a job for a newcomer, or one with little respect within the organisation.

- **'Middle-level managers'.** *Not necessarily full-time, but this group must be in the loop right from the outset. This group will deliver the operational changes required to move to CRM, so do not neglect their input. They (like the 'movers and shakers') do not need to attend every project meeting. Just keep them in the loop, and get their input on decisions that may affect them.*
- **Software vendor(s).** *How the software vendor is involved in the project team will depend on the vendor's project process. Whatever the arrangement, make sure the vendor at least gets the output from the project, delivered in a way the vendor will understand.*
- **Externals.** *For many firms, especially those approaching CRM for the first time, external providers, consultants, trainers etc, are part of an essential resource.*

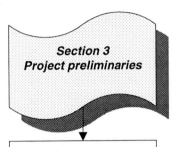

Section 3
Project preliminaries

Establishing the project team
Creating a balanced CRM team, and the composition of the team

Estimating CRM project costs
Typical project costs, and the likely cost areas: hardware, software and services, costs which are difficult to determine

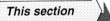

This section

Project risk - a high level view
Risks at the pre-launch and implementation stages

Introduction

It is rarely possible to state exactly what the total project cost is likely to be. There is however a need to offer a budgetary price, to give the management team some indication of:

a) The typical cost of CRM projects, of similar nature to the one planned
b) The likely cost areas
c) Costs that are difficult to determine
d) The impact of opportunity costs and management time

This section provides an indication of 'typical' costs and associated issues.

Price estimates are taken as at mid 2000. Given that software and hardware prices remain relatively stable (or actually fall in value-for-money terms), the effect of inflation should not be too great for the lifetime of the publication.

The typical cost of CRM projects

Costing CRM projects, indeed any IT project with its inherent complexity, is notoriously difficult. The answer to the cost question is … *'it all depends'*. It all depends on many factors. Even comparing projects that appear 'like for like', to understand how costs are derived is notoriously difficult. No two projects are so alike. Different companies choose to out-source different aspects of the project, and account for internal costs differently. One company may require a network upgrade to implement the CRM solution, another might have written off similar costs against a different project. In addition, for competitive reasons, few firms divulge the true cost of bringing their CRM strategy to fruition.

Therefore, on hearing of xyz Inc spending x amount on a CRM solution – don't expect your costs will be similar. The costs could be tens of thousands or hundreds of thousands. *It all depends.*

Managers need however a 'rule of thumb' to work with, at least to get a budget together. The following 'rule of thumb' diagram provides this. The costs used in the diagram include all cost elements, excluding hardware, i.e. software and services, as outlined in the section that follows.

'Rule of thumb' costing table

To use the diagram, follow the bottom axis showing the level of technical complexity. This axis goes from a simple network to a fully integrated system, one that 'automatically' integrates to an existing ERP system. On the left-hand axis identify the scope of the system – i.e. how many organisational boundaries the implementation crosses. The meeting point gives a very rough indicator of the likely 'per seat'[15] price – excluding hardware and associated network and IT infrastructure upgrade costs. For example, the rough cost of a sales and marketing solution, integrating to a 'best of breed' application, would be in the region of $7,000 (example A in the diagram.) Example B in the diagram indicates an approximate cost of $8,000 for an enterprise-wide solution, running on a network without integration.

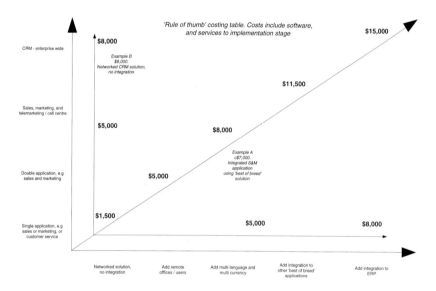

The likely cost areas

There are four main areas of cost:

- Hardware
- Software
- Services
- Support and maintenance.

If still at the project planning stage, it is unlikely that the variables for each area of cost are well enough identified. At this stage, it is probably only possible to produce an *indication* of the costs.

---

[15] 'per seat' is the IT market's way of saying 'per user'. Given that everyone is supposed to be mobile, and 'hot desking', and that 'location' counts for nothing anymore, 'per seat' seems a strange term to use!

The tables that follow outline either a) how the cost may be calculated or b) where the likely cost areas are.

Hardware costs

Hardware costs, at face value, appear to be the simplest to identify. Managers should be aware that the 'typical' CRM solution is very 'resource-hungry'. Often these systems require powerful PCs and (often several) powerful servers.

Equally, CRM solutions are bandwidth hungry, meaning that networks may require updating, simply to move data between integrated solutions and/or distant users.

The cost of hardware and bandwidth upgrades is therefore included in the section below on *'costs that are difficult to identify or determine'*. Non-technical managers, especially, need considerable technical support to determine these costs.

Hardware (excluding infrastructure upgrades)	
Laptop (with modem) for mobile users	Anything from £1,000 to £3,000 and up. Average costs around £1,900 for good specification machine, suitable for giving sales presentations on or for using as a web client, and heavy- duty applications.
Printer for laptop	Optional, and increasingly not used, given move towards the 'paperless office'. Expect to spend anything between £150 and £500 for a decent home/office printer.
Docking stations for office / mobile users	Allows remote users to dock with a base station in the office, expensive for what it is.

Software costs

Arriving at a price for software licences, with one or many vendors, should be straightforward. Should be, but is not. This is not a criticism of the software-vendor community, but another reflection of the complexity of the CRM project and the costing doctrine that simply states *'it all depends'*.

Generally, software vendors make it easy for their customers to begin an implementation in a small way, and add both users and functionality over time. This roll-out pricing is ideal, for example, where a project may benefit from implementing one user group first, with limited functionality as a pilot, then adding functionality and users over time.

It is this flexibility of roll out, and therefore of pricing, that makes accurate estimates difficult. Despite careful specification, there always seem to be additional modules available from the vendor that the project requires. So too, there always seem to be additional users needing access to the system, perhaps from additional departments, or simply because of a growth in the relevant departments. These factors alone may mean the eventual cost is different from the original estimate.

To reduce the risk of going over the estimate, remember that software-license pricing is usually on a volume-discount basis. Expect to pay more for early, low-volume licences – and negotiate well to receive retrospective discounts as the volume increases. Above all, get agreement on the volume-pricing structure well in advance, and make sure the vendor is in a position to stick to the deal offered.

To reduce the risk even more, remember that to buy specific functionality over and above 'base modules' can prove expensive. This is especially the case if vendors apply the full rate for a module to all users – even if only a percentage of users require the module. For example, many vendors provide 'telemarketing' modules as additional modules, or forecasting modules as additions. Their pricing models result in users in customer service or field sales paying for these modules, when they may not specifically require them.

The only way to avoid later difficulties in this area is to be absolutely sure of requirements, relative to the module-pricing structure applied by the vendor. Additionally, at an early a stage as possible, get as firm a commitment from the vendor regarding the pricing of ancillary modules. Specifically, ask vendors if there are any cost implications for users NOT requiring access to certain modules. – i.e. will they still be charged the full rate?

The following table provides an outline of cost considerations.

Software	
CRM application software	The hardest to estimate. Anything from £200 for a basic 'contact manager' to £8,000 for a fully featured CRM solution, per seat. See the 'rule of thumb' costing table, above, and associated comments.

continued

Services

Most projects include the use of external-service providers to a greater or lesser extent; for example, to provide services such as consultancy, training, project management etc. Therefore, service costs are given as person hours / degree of commitment or whatever factor is relevant. Managers can then adjust accordingly, to reflect the use of in-house or external resources and the size of the project.

Project management	In many cases, project management is outsourced because of the specialist nature of the work. For a major project (100 users plus) project management may be a full-time role, from inception right through to implementation. For medium-sized projects (50-100 users) allow 2-3 days per week average. For smaller projects (20-50 users) 1-2 days. Even the smallest projects (less than 20) still require at least ½ a day a week, to implementation and immediately beyond the roll-out.
Specification	A fully featured, organisation-wide system takes many hundreds of hours to specify. Often this work is shared between vendor, business-process consultant, and the end users' project team. Anticipate that before the roll out or even the pilot, 75% of the effort is to go into developing and signing off the specification. Elapsed time is often the factor with specification. For major systems, allow *minimum* 4-6 months, smaller systems *minimum* 2-4 months, and even the smallest system takes an elapsed time of 1 month to specify. Actual hours is more dependent on the system / vendor and process complexity, plus how quickly managers take to agree to the specification.
Selection	Including negotiation and due diligence investigations; as a rule of thumb the selection process may take about the same time as the specification process. However, it can run in parallel to this.
Configuration	Actual hours for configuration is dependent on the system / vendor and the process complexity. Configuration involves taking what comes out of the box[16] and setting it up to meet the needs of the business. The bigger the user community, the harder and more complex and time-consuming this is. As a rule of thumb, assume at least 2-3 days elapsed time per user group / department and significant process – assuming the vendor has sufficient resources to complete the configuration work. For example, field sales is one 'group', account managers is a group, campaign management is a process, managing in-bound customer care calls is a process. For example, 30 significant processes would take about 70 person days configuration and cost accordingly.
Costs for pilot(s)	At this stage, the project team need to know about 'opportunity costs' associated with pilots and, indeed, all activity relating to the implementation – see below. These opportunity costs can be significant – so make sure to include them in the 'buy in' presentation. Bear in mind that, to complete the pilot, the project will need to absorb the costs of specification and configuration – or there won't be any software to pilot.
Training and roll-out	Of all implementation service costs, training costs are probably the easiest to estimate. And, at this stage, the project team need to know that training is a direct cost (i.e. to pay external trainers) plus possibly opportunity costs – see above. External trainers typically cost about £800-£1500 per day, *plus set-up costs and course development*. Allow ratio 1 trainer to 8 delegates.

---

[16] 'Out of the box'. The software industry's term for something which is useless but comes straight 'out of the box'; it is basically software that needs setting up to do what you want it to do – i.e. configuration.

Course length minimum 1 day, typical 2 days, extreme (but necessary, in some cases, 5 days.) A 64-user system would require say 16 training days (2 days, 8 delegates per course) plus set up and course development. Course set up and development costs are about 6 times the duration of the course –more if complex processes need explaining. So set up would be 8 x 2 days = 16 days. Plus allow time / money for validating the training process with the relevant operational managers, and 'train the trainer' courses – typically another 7 – 10 days.

In some cases, however, the costs are so specific they can only be calculated in conjunction with the project specification, such as the cost of configuration and running pilots. Where possible, these costs are shown as a % of the total project costs. However, these are only estimates and, as previously stated, every project is different – and '*it all depends...*'

Maintenance and support

Maintenance costs include both direct and indirect or, internal costs. Direct costs are easier to calculate, being set as a percentage of the software licences. However, even this is complex, since these costs should be in line with any roll-out schedule, and applied accordingly as the project rolls out. More difficult to estimate are the indirect costs of internal support personnel.

During the early stages of rolling out, the CRM solution users, typically, need considerable support to help them on a day-to-day basis. Much of this can be out-sourced, for example, for a period immediately after the implementation using an external resource to help bed down the solution. This is not cost effective or satisfactory as a long-term solution. In the long term, CRM solutions need their own internal resource, to be sure of achieving the vision.

The table that follows provides an estimate of the likely internal resource requirement.

Costs which are difficult to determine or identify

Determining the project cost on a 'Greenfield' site, with no existing users, no existing technical infrastructure, no existing systems, would be relatively straightforward. Normally, CRM systems are implemented where there exists a variety of systems, data, users and numerous factors that make it difficult to accurately project the total cost from the outset.

Implementing a solution onto the existing infrastructure involves 3 main areas of costs that are difficult to determine:

Maintenance and support	
CRM Application software maintenance	Software maintenance negotiable with the vendor. Expect to pay between 15% and 20% of the licence fee, to keep the software current and have bugs fixed.
CRM Application support	Software application support negotiable with the vendor. Expect to pay between 15% and 20% of the licence fee, to have online support from the vendor.
End-user support – business processes	Once the system is 'live', users need a point of reference to confirm their use of new system/process combinations is correct, and to get day-to-day support. Large systems allow 3-5 people full time per week until system is running well, smaller system 1-3 persons full time. For smallest systems, still allow ½ day per week.
End-user support – application technical support	The CRM will be another product for the internal IT team to support. Workload difficult to determine; remember that many users, especially if they are getting PCs for the first time, will require considerable support – often based mainly out of the office.
Hardware support and maintenance	Provided via hardware manufacture. Negotiable, and may be included in part of existing IT support contracts; check with IT dept.

continued

1) Upgrades to the technical infrastructure
2) Data conversion
3) Interfaces to legacy or other systems

These costs are very project-specific, and few CRM projects of any significance do not involve expenditure in these areas.

The impact of opportunity costs and the costs of management time

'Opportunity cost' is the term given to the cost of not doing one thing because of doing another.

For example, sales people cannot be selling if they are attending a training session to learn about using the new CRM solution. The productivity of marketing might dip during implementation of new campaign-management processes, and so on across all departments. Managers, already working to capacity, will have to divert their efforts away from their 'normal' work, if the implementation of the CRM is to be successful. These opportunity costs are not to be underestimated. They represent the amount of time and effort required during the

Hardware upgrade	Existing users may require more powerful PCs to run the processor and memory-hungry CRM application. For infrequent users, the cost of upgrading the PC may be out of all proportion to the business benefit of the solution.
Network upgrade	Many CRM applications are 'bandwidth[17] hungry', especially those running over WANs.[18]
Communications infrastructure upgrade	The CRM solution, connecting as it does numerous departments, may require a significant upgrade to the communications infrastructure as these users begin to communicate for the first time.
Additional users	The wider the system boundary gets … the wider the system boundary gets! As the application grows, there are nearly always additional users needing access, and they all need a licence and to be connected.
Data conversion and cleaning	Existing data needs cleaning and being made ready for the new system. Data may be held in numerous databases across the organisation. Cleaning data takes time (and costs).
Integrating legacy or any other system[19]	The cost of integrating to old systems is almost impossible to estimate. Not least, opening up an old system can reveal a need to fix the old system, prior to thinking about integration. Therefore, do not expect that just because there is data in a system, it is immediately useable in the CRM solution.
Bespoke software writing	By definition, an unknown entity. Usually very expensive, time-consuming, costly to maintain, and generally carries a high-risk factor. On the other hand, bespoke software (in some cases by its very nature) may provide significant competitive advantage, at least in the short term. Don't automatically write off the bespoke or, more likely, semi-bespoke solution. It is normally beneficial to undertake a **separate** ROI exercise on the bespoke element of the solution.

implementation by managers, which must be taken from their normal activity.

In particular, opportunity costs may be high if a firm is implementing a CRM solution for the first time. First-time system users need more training, take longer to adapt to new processes, and usually require more management effort to get a good return on the investment.

---

[17] Bandwidth = a measure of capacity - and therefore means how quickly and how much data moves through the cable.

[18] WAN = Wide Area Network. A network of PCs connected, but located widely apart – e.g. different office locations. Contrasts with a LAN, a Local Area Network, where the machines are typically in the same building.

[19] Legacy system = a system still in use, but soon to be made redundant. In the IT world, this frequently means anything more than a couple of versions old!

On the other hand, firms implementing a CRM solution for the first time do generally have the biggest gains to make.

Management 'costs' reflect the time managers put into a project of this nature. Whilst a lot of work can be out-sourced (which, of course, has an impact on direct costs), managers still need to allocate significant amounts of time to the CRM project.

The requirement on management time needs discussing right at the inception of the project. This is a fundamental part of the 'buy-in' process – especially due to the cross-organisational nature of the project. Managers in all departments need to be aware that their departments will benefit from the CRM solution – but they must do their bit towards the success of the project. This means allocating the scarcest resource of all – time.

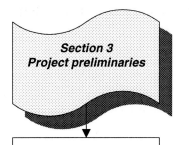

**Section 3
Project preliminaries**

**Establishing the project
team**
Creating a balanced CRM
team, and the composition
of the team

**Estimating CRM project
costs**
Typical project costs, and
the likely cost areas:
hardware, software and
services, costs which are
difficult to determine

This section

**Project risk - a high level
view**
Risks at the pre-launch
and implementation
stages

Introduction

There are numerous references available to the manager on project-risk management. Therefore, this section does not provide a guide to project-risk management *per se*.

Rather, the section is concerned with outlining to the CRM project manager the key issues that should be included in the project plan about a range of risks. In identifying these key issues, part of the aim is to help the manager reduce the overall risk – through more thorough preparation.

To summarise this section, an appropriate and well-known adage would be *'failing to plan is planning to fail'*. If the CRM project manager fails to adequately plan the following areas, there is a high chance the CRM project will fail.

The eventual CRM project plan should include reference to the following risk issues, in the context of:

- Elapsed time to complete the launch-project stage
- Contingency planning
- Risk-reduction strategies
- Resource allocation

CRM high-level project risks at phase 1 – pre-launch

Check for changes to the organisational structure and distribution channel.

Some managers may not be so close to the CRM project, and may underestimate the impact of distribution channel changes and organisational structure changes on the project. Make sure the plan includes specific reference to the likelihood of any changes in this and associated areas, for example, planned merger and acquisition and changes to the structure of the sales force or channel strategy. These, in particular, have massive implications for managing customer relationships – and therefore the CRM project.

Of course, the CRM strategy may force such change, which is a different issue, and these risks should be assessed at the strategy stage of the project.

Cross-check with IT department to identify any other resource-grabbing projects.

What other projects the IT department are supporting during the planned CRM implementation should be revealed during the 'buy-in phase'. Nevertheless, the CRM project plan must reference the overall IT project plan. Resource-grabbing projects can overlap, and potentially rob the CRM project manager of valuable IT resources – at precisely the wrong time.

In particular watch for network upgrades, new 'back-office' projects and data-warehouse projects. All these not only drain IT resources, but are also likely to overlap from a technical perspective because of the use of similar data sets. At the very least, having an awareness of these projects can significantly reduce the risk.

Cross-check with every other department (for other resource-grabbing projects or seasonal events or business cycles).

Similar to checking the IT project plan, the CRM project plan must reference key sales, marketing and customer-service activity. For example, planning extensive CRM system training, immediately before an end-of-year sales' push, is never a good idea. Planning to implement a new 'campaign-management process', in the middle of several product launches, is unlikely to help marketing.

Often it is difficult to avoid potential clashes in the schedule. However, knowing about potential clashes puts the manager in a far stronger position to implement good risk-reduction strategies.

CRM project risk at phase 2 – prior to implementation

System specification – producing process maps
This requires extensive access to users and managers. In practice, what this means is that for every user group the elapsed time to complete the specification increases, as it takes time to document needs. Correspondingly, the greater the elapsed time the higher the risk of having to change the specification, as users' needs change and the elapsed time to complete the specification increases.

In this scenario, we see the dynamic nature of the CRM project dramatically increasing the risk of designing a system which is out of date well before it comes into use. There are two associated risks to guard against. Firstly, lack of access to managers within a reasonable time-scale may mean that the eventual specification does not fit users' needs, since there may be insufficient time to complete this work correctly. Secondly, lack of access means the specification phase drags on, delaying the project and risking not gaining an early enough / strong enough competitive advantage.

This always seems to take longer than planned – or perhaps uninformed managers fail to plan enough time! Even when mapping process in an efficient CRM project document managers still need time to read, understand, and sign off 'their' processes. Do not expect managers to do this overnight. Anticipate that, understandably, managers may require more time before agreeing to the 'final' specification.

The project plan needs to allow time for both preparing the brief for vendors, and for vendors to make a considered response. Any half-decent vendor will need at least a few weeks to produce a half-decent response. Make sure there is enough elapsed time for several iterations of the briefing process. The bigger the project, the more iterations, and the greater the likelihood that several vendors will be involved. Don't risk making an ill-informed decision, simply for lack of planning enough time far enough in advance.

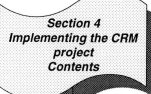

**Section 4
Implementing the CRM
project
Contents**

Project phases
Why CRM projects never
end, the different
approaches required for
each stage, and the core
project threads

**Mapping the CRM vision
to the project**
Putting the software
element into context,
producing a project launch
document, defining and
signing-off user
requirements

**Configuring and piloting
the solution**
Building a prototype, and
planning and managing
both conference room
pilots and field pilots.
Managing pilot feedback,
piloting the training
solution

**Data migration and
integration**
The operational challenge
of CRM data, finding and
using suitable data,
making sure everything
goes smoothly

Section 4 – Implementation

This section concerns the process of creating something which represents the organisation's vision for CRM, a phase that requires managers to remember that 'the devil is in the detail'.

Users will expect that the solution reflects the detail relating to their working practices – and managers will expect that the detailed outputs they require from the solution are available. In addition, there are numerous details relating to data, project management, training, and a whole raft of operational details to get right.

An analogy would be that of building foundations. Get the foundations right, and the building is safe. Get foundations wrong and not only will the building be insecure – it will be very hard to go back and alter them, once they are in place.

**Section 4
Implementing the CRM
project**

Project phases
Why CRM projects never
end, the different
approaches required for
each stage, and the core
project threads

This section

**Mapping the CRM vision
to the project**
Putting the software
element into context,
producing a project launch
document, defining and
signing-off user
requirements

**Configuring and piloting
the solution**
Building a prototype, and
planning and managing
both conference room
pilots and field pilots.
Managing pilot feedback,
piloting the training
solution

**Data migration and
integration**
The operational challenge
of CRM data, finding and
using suitable data,
making sure everything
goes smoothly

When will the project end?

In the project-planning process, *'how long do CRM projects last?'* is an often-repeated question. As if the project has a start point, a middle point and an end point, managers are keen to know when they can say 'we've done CRM'- and then safely move onto something new. But, in reality, CRM projects never actually finish. Certainly, they have a start point and a peak workload during the main implementation phase, but they do not actually 'finish'. This is because CRM is about a change in the culture of the organisation, a battle for 'hearts and minds', and a shift in the way the organisation interacts with its customers. It is not surprising, therefore, that there is no specific 'end date' – CRM should be a state of mind for the organisation – not something to start and then stop, over the course of a year or two.

Rather, a CRM project needs thinking about in three distinct phases.

The three phases of a 'never-ending' CRM project

A more effective approach is to see the CRM project as a three-phase process – where the 'final' phase is one of continuous improvement, striving to ensure a return on the investment and true cultural change. Framing the complete CRM project in this way helps to influence both the approach and project team structure, for each of the three phases. In fact, each phase requires a significantly different attitude and approach (and therefore management skill-set) to achieve the optimum result for the phase, as illustrated in the diagram below.

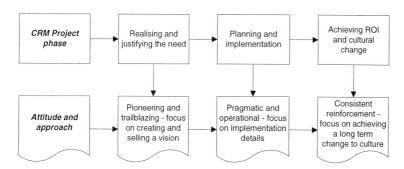

Different 'attitudes and approaches' required at each project phase

At the beginning of the project (realising and justifying the need), there is a need for managers to galvanise the organisation into action, and see that the project starts correctly. At the next stage (planning and implementation), a slightly different skill-set is required. For the implementation phase, managers need to be aware of the detail, focusing on bringing all the many different aspects of the project together; the role is more project manager than visionary. Post implementation, the project benefits by a further style (achieving ROI and cultural change); managers must ensure a long-term return, and concentrate on ensuring that the planned cultural and strategic changes happen.

Understanding the long-term nature of CRM sets the scene for an understanding of the overall project process. Approaching the project in this way helps managers to ensure long-term success. That is, an enterprise-wide improvement in managing customer relationships – rather than simple short-term operational gain.

Project threads

Whilst the CRM project may have no end date, it does include a number of distinct project threads. These interrelate, forming numerous dependencies, the distinct project threads being:

CRM project process, and implementing change
- Managing the CRM project team
- Managing cultural change
- Managing operational change
- Mapping business process to solution

Vendor and resource-related issues
- Vendor and solution selection
- Contractual issues and vendor performance
- Managing other external resources
- Managing other internal resources

Technical issues
- Technical infrastructure selection and management
- Data migration
- Integration to other systems
- Other technical issues

Roll-out issues
- Training and documentation
- Pilot(s)
- Managing feedback
- Roll out
- Other roll-out issues
- Ongoing support, development and maintenance
- Post roll-out activity

Good practice in CRM project management (in fact in all project management) requires the creation of a project plan, to manage each of the project threads. It is important to frame the project in the context of the main factors likely to impact on the overall success; the main success factors in this case being:

Project threads

	Achievement of the vision	Achievement of required ROI	Risk management	Resource and budget management	Managing project dependencies	Managing project timescales
CRM project process and implementing change						
Managing the CRM project team						
Managing cultural change						
Managing operational change						
Mapping process to solution						
Vendor and resource related issues						
Vendor and solution selection						
Contractual issues and vendor performance			Project threads and context			
Managing other external resources						
Managing other internal resources						
Technical issues						
Technical infrastructure - selection and management						
Data migration						
Integration to other systems						
Other technical issues						
Roll-out issues						
Training and documentation						
Pilot(s)						
Managing feedback						
Roll-out						
Other roll-out issues						
Ongoing support development and maintenance						
Post roll-out activity						

Project context

Mapping project threads, into the context of the project

For simplicity and clarity, the process diagram shown below excludes dependencies and the interrelation between process steps.

Map project to CRM vision	Undertake resource selection process	Confirm actual phasing and roll out timing	Complete trial configuration of solution	Confirm plan for pilot(s)	Complete pilot(s)	Plan roll-out phases	Complete roll-out phases
Identify process / and solution needs	Select solution and vendor	Initiate planning for pilot(s)	Test data migration to trial configuration	Plan pilot training, produce documentation	Act on pilot feedback	Plan roll out training	Training and documentation
Identify key technical issues and resource requirements	Select technical solution and partners	Plan data migration	Test data integration to trial configuration	Plan pilot feedback process	Verify fit between process and vision	Complete roll out documentation	Data migration
Confirm desired phasing and roll out timing	Identify need for, and select, other external resources	Plan integration	Verify changes made / planned to technical infrastructure	Plan technical implementation for pilot, and support resources	Verify change management program	Plan live data migration	Data integration
Establish change management program	Identify need for, and locate, other internal resources	Plan changes to technical infrastructure	Verify change management program	Produce high level roll out plan		Plan live integration	Change management, continuous program

Continue with strategy to achieve ROI and desired vision / cultural change

Address cultural change issues

- Achievement of the vision
- Achievement of the required return on investment
- Risk management
- Resource and budget management
- Managing project dependencies
- Managing project time scales

This provides a structure for monitoring and reporting on the project. In turn, this provides a framework for more mundane activities, such as producing meeting agendas and collating management reports. It is useful to produce a 'matrix' report to illustrate the project progression, mapping each *thread* against the main '*project context*'. In particular, such a matrix helps managers to highlight issues before they become problematic, and ensure that important issues are not left unresolved from one review period to the next.

There follows a further diagram illustrating (shown over the page; again at a high-level) the CRM project process. The diagram shows the project process in a chronological sequence, from initiation through to completing the roll-out process. The purpose of this diagram is to identify some of the specific tasks associated with each phase.

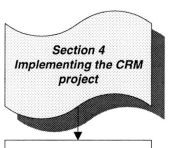

Section 4
Implementing the CRM
project

Project phases
Why CRM projects never
end, the different
approaches required for
each stage, and the core
project threads

Mapping the CRM vision
to the project
Putting the software
element into context,
producing a project launch
document, defining and
signing-off user
requirements

This section

Configuring and piloting
the solution
Building a prototype, and
planning and managing
both conference room
pilots and field pilots.
Managing pilot feedback,
piloting the training
solution

Data migration and
integration
The operational challenge
of CRM data, finding and
using suitable data,
making sure everything
goes smoothly

Mapping CRM processes

It is essential to define the required business process so that end-users and non-technical personnel alike understand what should happen to achieve the vision of CRM. Only when this is complete is it possible to configure the technical CRM solution to help manage the business processes. At the same time, it is important to remember that the 'CRM solution' must include far more than the software, if the solution is to help achieve the vision and the associated cultural change.

The process mapping must ensure a close and continuing relationship between strategic vision and the implementation of 'the solution'. Without this close relationship, CRM is nothing more than the implementation of a few software tools and operational changes to achieve some process efficiencies. Consequently, the vision is lost.

Therefore, the process mapping must take a *holistic* view of CRM. Holistic means looking across the *whole* organisation and, in the case of CRM, beyond the organisation towards both customers and suppliers.

You cannot load cultural change from a CD or access it over a computer network, but the temptation when implementing a software solution is to assume this is possible. Managers see a magical box of CRM tricks, full of software wizardry. 'Can it do this?' 'Can it do that?' they ask of the software vendor. Obligingly, the vendor points out that yes, it can.

Managers, sold on the hype of CRM, see the software solution as the source for all positive change. Everything that was ever broken in the organisation will miraculously be fixed through this new amazing piece of CRM technology – right?

Wrong.

The mistake many managers make is to assume that every single piece of change, needed to move the organisation to the CRM vision is contained in the software solution. It is not, and never will be.

What process mapping should do, therefore, is illustrate precisely:

a)   What the software is to provide
b)   What managers must do to achieve the vision

Making the vision of CRM understandable

To realise the CRM vision, users must see the impact on how they work on a daily basis, and what achieving the vision means to them. The vision therefore needs to be explicit and understandable. To provide this clarity of definition, a sensible approach is to create a 'launch document' outlining the specific intentions of the project.

The document must illustrate the requirements for the associated *cultural* and *operational* changes, together with the technical requirements of the solution.

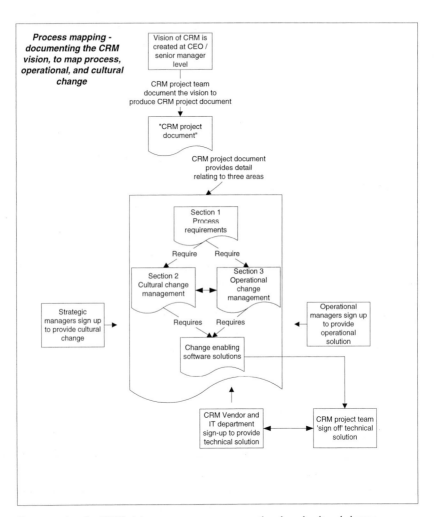

Documenting the CRM vision, to map process, operational, and cultural change

The CRM project document emphasises the need for change in three areas:

- Technological
- Operational
- Cultural

The main criteria for the CRM project launch document are:

- Explicitly link vision and solution – remembering that the 'solution' is not simply the software
- Document by processes – not by organisational 'silos'
- Involve the management team in the production of the document
- Create a document that accommodates change. ***In the launch document, create an explicit link between the vision for CRM and the CRM technical solution***

The link between CRM vision and CRM solution is the very essence of the CRM project challenge. Users need to know ***why*** things are changing. They need to understand the relationship between a perceived software feature and the organisational strategy for CRM.

Create a process-driven view – not a 'silo-focused' view

CRM must encourage cross-departmental co-operation – in contrast to the 'silo' approach to sales, marketing and customer service, where everything belongs to a department first, and an organisational process second.

Therefore the launch document must drill down to each 'significant' process – examining ***how the process operates first***, and what each department does second. For example, the process of 'enquiry generation and lead handling' involves many sub-processes and touches many departments. Describe this from the perspective of the process first, and the departmental responsibility second. At the same time, highlight how the proposed changes to the process move the organisation towards the vision of CRM, i.e. the associated cultural change.

Involve many managers in the creation of the launch document

Launching a CRM project is not a job for an individual since the CRM processes belongs to the whole organisation.

Working in teams produces work that is far more relevant, far more quickly than relying on one individual. Additionally, of course, working in teams helps with the 'buy-in' process. Team members quickly begin the process of educating the wider organisation (and themselves) about the meaning of CRM. Teams should be grouped around cross-organisational processes.

Create a launch document that is easy to change

Because of the dynamic nature of the environment, the implementation must embrace change within the project process. This includes producing a CRM project process that is easily adapted and changed. Moreover, it must be simple to identify changes as they happen, i.e. to reference these changes in the documentation.

Process mapping – example

The diagram below illustrates an example of a 'high-level' process map. In this case, the process concerns: 'Key Account Management' (KAM).

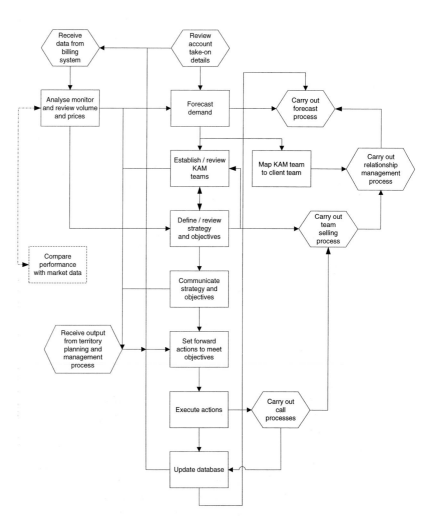

Example of a Key Account Management process, produced for a CRM implementation

In the example, assume that 'Key Account Management' is a new concept for the organisation, as it moves towards a CRM strategy. In view of the introduction of Key Account Management, the CRM process-mapping document must highlight all of the related CRM issues – both technical and the cultural and organisational changes required to implement CRM.

The following is an example of the issues that might be included in the launch document, based on the diagram above. In reality, there will be many other requirements, in addition to those noted below. The example is not intended to provide an exhaustive list of the requirements of CRM in Key Account Management. Each requirement is referenced (in parenthesis at the end of the requirement) as mainly associated with technical, operational or cultural changes, or a combination of these.

Forecast demand

Demands forecasting in the CRM environment is complex. Not least, the model of forecasting suggested for good CRM includes reference to the external market. This provides a far more accurate picture than simply referencing the internal views of those managers contributing to the forecast. In addition, it makes sense to map the forecast onto the actual result, to a) verify the accuracy of the forecast and, b) identify where the organisation is failing to win business.

The CRM launch material would need to reference the requirement to:

- Set the demand forecast in the context of the market – requiring data from an external market analysis, and probably a reassessment of the organisation's segmentation strategy – potentially required to match the data available from the market analysis *(technical and operational)*
- Provide training to sales personnel, to help them interpret and act on the forecast *(cultural and operational)*
- Store past forecast data to enable an assessment of forecast accuracy and variance over time *(mostly technical)*
- Interface to the sales order-processing system, to provide sales people with a view of performance vs forecast. The account records in the sales order-processing system and the existing sales database may not be the same, requiring a data-cleaning exercise before roll out. This is equally a technical and operational database-cleaning exercise *(technical and operational)*
- Be flexible – to enable the reworking of the forecast as sales areas change *(technical)*

Review data from billing systems

Many organisations have sales order-processing and billing data in one area, and CRM-related data in another. Bringing the two together is fraught with difficulty. Not least, many firms find it hard to reconcile the account record, of the sales person's physical calls, with the purchasing account.

The CRM launch material would need to reference the requirement to:

- Provide an analysis of the billing data, to enable account managers to use this information productively, give training to account managers on interpreting the data relative to market performance, and produce forecast data per account *(technical and operational)*
- Interface the billing system and the CRM system – allowing for credits and returns as well as sales data *(technical)*
- Allow accounts personnel and sales personnel to share the sales data connected with any account, bringing together account-data records and sales-data records *(operational and cultural)*
- Map sales data (for example, recorded only by product number) into the product groups used in marketing and sales *(technical)*

KAM teams

The technical aspect of the CRM solution generally offers functionality to enable a sales organisation to work in teams, sharing activity and contact data on groups of accounts. Working in teams enables the organisation to share the account-management workload over several account managers. Not least, the benefits include the potential to leverage the knowledge of an account more effectively to increase the revenue from associated accounts. For an organisation to move to the model of 'team selling' requires far more openness and transparency than individual selling, and is therefore fraught with the difficulties of change management.

The CRM process-mapping document would need to reference the requirement to:

- Identify groups of accounts by associations such as 'parent / child' *(technical and operational)*
- Create sales teams and map these to groups of accounts *(mostly cultural)*
- Consider the applicability of the existing reward structure (at the moment focused on the individual). Is a team-reward structure more appropriate? *(operational and very cultural)*
- Change the perception 'individual's own accounts', to demonstrate that the company 'owns' the accounts, and all should share account information *(cultural and operational)*

- Provide an understanding to the sales team concerning the concepts of 'leverage' and 'team selling' *(operational and cultural)*
- Ensure a fit between the team structure and the use of the forecasting element of CRM *(technical, operational, and cultural)*

What this process mapping reveals

The extract from the mapping exercise above covers just a few of the process steps across one aspect of the CRM implementation – Key Account Management. However, even this short exercise reveals many technical, cultural and operational issues the organisation must face to implement CRM successfully. Not least, these include major areas, such as a move towards team selling and sharing account information. This could lead to a possible change to the reward scheme (in this case to encompass team-based rewards). These issues alone can bring the CRM project grinding to a halt – as managers feel threatened by greater transparency and the threat to established pay and conditions.

This example should illustrate the considerable benefit of undertaking this wider form of process mapping, i.e. to include a consideration of the cultural and the operational sooner rather than later. Doing this sooner at least reveals the potential issues likely to require management attention as the project comes to fruition and allows the management team time to address the issues. Leaving many of these issues (especially the cultural and operational) until a week before the roll out of 'the solution' would obviously be disastrous for the CRM strategy. And, understandably, managers would feel cheated if they did not have enough time to prepare to implement the vision and address these wider issues.

Section 4
Implementing the CRM
project

Project phases
Why CRM projects never
end, the different
approaches required for
each stage, and the core
project threads

**Mapping the CRM vision
to the project**
Putting the software
element into context,
producing a project launch
document, defining and
signing-off user
requirements

**Configuring and piloting
the solution**
Building a prototype, and
planning and managing
both conference room
pilots and field pilots.
Managing pilot feedback,
piloting the training
solution

This section

**Data migration and
integration**
The operational challenge
of CRM data, finding and
using suitable data,
making sure everything
goes smoothly

Introduction

This section covers work associated with configuring the software solution and running a series of pilots. To achieve this, it is essential to have managers able to act as 'process professionals' and take ownership of the CRM solution.

On the three-phase project model this work sits within the implementation phase, as indicated below. Configuration is however an ongoing activity, especially in the dynamic CRM environment. Once the configuration stops, either the CRM environment solution or the organisation is in decline, because both solution and culture will have stopped responding to changes in the external environment.

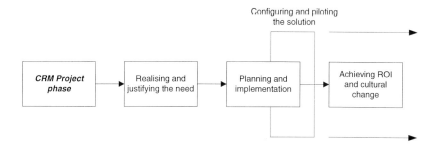

Configuring and piloting the solution within the project model

As with other phases, it is essential during this phase to make progress on more than one front. On the one hand, the software requires configuring to fit user needs. On the other hand, this phase represents a time when the project team must make the organisation aware of what CRM means in practice. In addition, it must be made clear to managers the responsibility they have, to help ensure the success of the CRM strategy.

Understanding 'configuration'

In this context 'configuration' means changing the software element of the CRM solution (technically, of course, it is not a solution until after the configuration is complete and all components are in place) to fit the specific needs of the organisation. Configuration is necessary because the 'out-of-the-box' version of the solution is unlikely to arrive with precisely the correct configuration. The 'out-of-the-box' solution will have a standard set of fields, such as those concerned with contact details, names and addresses, and some standard fields for example, to record meetings and visits. Most firms need to add to these fields, and / or make the fields specific to their organisation, and / or make fields behave in a particular way to fit the business process.

In an ideal world, the software solution is configurable in many areas; these are outlined below, starting with the database structure.

Database configuration

To complete the configuration it is necessary to compare the fields in the 'out-of-the-box' solution with the fields identified as being required, through the earlier analysis. Then, have the fields added as required. In practice, configuration is becoming increasingly easy in modern CRM solutions – although there may be some limitations, depending on the underlying structure or make-up of the database. Generally, the more complex the software offering, the greater potential to configure.

The steps are:

1. Compare the structure of the basis with that required (see diagram over the page)
2. Amend the structure of the database to fit the business need
3. Compare the fields with the database with that required
4. Amend the database fields as required
5. Compare screen views (i.e. what appears on the screens)
6. Amend as required
7. Construct different views for different users and user groups (see below)
8. Add 'business rules', including rules relating to security
9. Test and sense check the configuration
10. Tidy as required

This over-course is a vast oversimplification of what is an extremely complex process. A process which may take months from start to finish, involve numerous iterations, sense checks, and lots of time and effort – i.e. much more than the simple 10-step process shown above suggests.

A good starting point

Since 'contact management' is the basis of all CRM solutions, contact management is a good starting point to illustrate the configuration process.

A typical database configuration, for a 'contact-manager' solution might be as defined in the diagram below. In addition to the basic structure of Company, Contacts and Activities, this structure includes

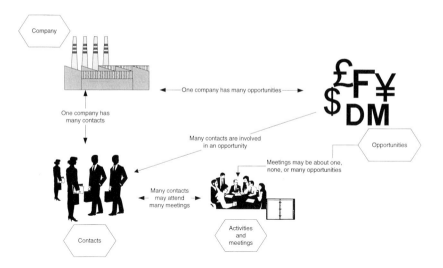

Basic Contact Manager structure

'opportunities'. Although less common in the contact manager, the inclusion of 'opportunities' represents a typical scenario. The terms one-to-many, one-to-one and many-to-many describe the relationships between the entities in the database. (The entities contain the main tables in the database, where each table holds a certain category of information.)

After considering the database structure, the next step is to consider the database fields. In this example, the 'out-of-the-box' table for contacts might include the following fields:

Field	*Examples*
Title	Mr, Mrs, Miss
Initial	P
Surname	Smith
First Name	Paul
Salutation	Dear Paul
Job Code	Marketing
Job Description Services	Head of Marketing
Level in organisation	2 – 1 below CEO
Direct 'phone	9999 99999 99999
Mobile	9999 99999 99999
Head office direct	9999 99999 99999
E-mail	pauls@telco.com

The configuration generally requires supplementing with company-specific information. In the example below, a company in the telecoms sector adds some fields specifically to meet their requirements:

Field	*Examples*
Influence on choice of ISP	High, Medium, Low
Influence on choice of voice services	High, Medium, Low
Influence on choice of data service	High, Medium, Low
Influence on telecoms strategy	High, Medium, Low
Warmth to Telco.com	Very warm, Medium, Dislikes
Home teleco	BT
Home ISP	Direct Connection

It is the addition of new fields (and probably new tables) that is the basis of the work required to configure the database element of the software, for example, to extend the database structure and add many functional routines to support a more complex scenario, a scenario which is more typical for a CRM implementation.

In the more complex scenario:

1. It is not unusual for a database diagram of an 'out-of-the-box' solution to be printed on poster-size paper (a pin up for the technically minded!)
2. The field list runs into several thousands
3. The relationships between fields and tables are extremely complex
4. The addition of rules to support bespoke business processes adds complexity, making the technical definition difficult to understand
5. The addition of functional routines such as forecasting, reporting, campaign management, customer-service, incident tracking etc adds more complexity. These functional routines are made up of data, coupled with processes, and different screens to present the data to the user

In addition to configuring the database tables and fields, it is generally necessary to configure several other areas, as outlined below:

Screen layout – where a field is to appear on a screen. Without being able to position where a field appears on the screen, the solution may capture the required data, but be difficult and not intuitive for the users to use.

Code tables – what options users are to select, to use in a particular field.

Field types – to configure how a data field is used, for example as a 'free-text' field where the user may make any entry, as a number field or a currency field, or as a field using a selection from a code table.

Mandatory / non-mandatory – where the solution forces or does not force the user to make an entry before the database record can be saved.

User groups and security – in most cases, it is necessary to configure which users have access to which screens, and / or fields and processes. There are two reasons for this. Firstly, to restrict access to sensitive data that only certain users should see. Secondly, to remove functionality from users who don't need it, and where its addition makes it more difficult to use the solution.

Field-level security – to determine whether a user or user group has permission to add, edit or delete data within a particular field or group of fields.

Process functions – for example, an automated and sequential process to manage a series of fields that guide the user to complete a specific task.

Access to external programs and documents – for example, to give users access to, or restrict users from other software packages such as MS Office, e-mail clients with the CRM solution.

Report and data extraction – the security and field-data configuration must take account of how users are to tract data and obtain reports from the solution.

Configuration and the bespoke solution

To understand the limitations of any configuration process, it is important to define what is meant by 'configuration'. For our purposes configuration must mean:

To change the out-of-the-box package within defined parameters, using standard functions within the package to make the changes. To be called 'configuration'changes, and the resulting configuration must be supported and maintained through upgrade versions, by the software vendor on standard terms.

This definition of configuration is important, since it separates configuration from producing a bespoke addition or amending a standard solution, in a bespoke way.

Bespoke

Using the working definition of configuration, given above, it is relevant to say of bespoke software that it:

- Alters the out-of-the-box solution in a non-standard way
- Will require additional documentation, specifically to integrate the bespoke element into the standard solution
- Will require specific arrangements for support, to ensure the vendors' help desk is able to support the client's bespoke element of the solution and especially how the bespoke element interacts with the-out-of- the-box element of the solution
- Will require specific arrangements for upgrades, to ensure the bespoke element is supportable through modifications and upgrades to the out-of-the-box solution

If the CRM project requires bespoke software, then so be it. Managers must however understand the difference in the risk profile between configuration and bespoke work, and approach the proposed changes to the out-of-the-box solution accordingly.

However, it is sometimes difficult for the client to separate 'configuration' from 'bespoke'. This is because in some cases the vendor may prefer to describe 'bespoke' work as 'configuration' – to avoid increasing the risk profile of their proposition. This can have serious consequences, and therefore it is essential to know from the outset how the vendor intends to adapt the out-of-the-box solution to meet any client-specific requirements.

One of the reasons for accepting a bespoke solution (or part-bespoke solution) is the potential to achieve competitive advantage, using innovative CRM solutions. In some cases, the very nature of a bespoke addition provides something that is different from what the competitor has. Assuming that this adds value to the business in a way that others in the market do not, there is increased potential for competitive advantage.

Consequences of changing the configuration

The configuration develops through several iterations, with input from several managers, coordinated by the process professionals. During this stage, the project team must collate the requested configuration changes made via each process professional. However, one change may cancel out another – or worse, a change may have an overall negative impact on the solution. This is because CRM-related processes are so integrated it is difficult to alter one part of the integrated solution without impacting on another.

Therefore, the iterative process must include a review by the CRM project team. The aim is to complete the configuration quickly, accurately, and with the minimum of bureaucracy.

A common problem with amendments to the configuration is in the use of a 'code' selection in a particular field. Different departments may need to use the same field in a different part of the process. Because of this, there is potential for codes to conflict. For example, one department may wish the field to be compulsory, whilst another may not be in a position to add any data at all.

Therefore, to aid the change process the ideal is to **map each field with each process**. In this way, it is possible to identify which processes use which fields, and where the likely areas of conflict are.

Making and sticking to decisions

Many configuration decisions have an impact beyond the operation of the CRM solution. For example:

- Decisions on how a forecasting module operates may have an impact on pay and rewards
- Decisions about campaign-management functions may impact on allocating work loads
- Decisions on team selling may change the relationship between which sales person 'owns' an account

One of the problems faced by the CRM project team, however, is that managers are often slow to make these policy decisions. Alternatively, they expect the decisions they make one week can be undone the next.

Procrastination and changing direction is a real danger to the success of the CRM project. Specifically, procrastination makes it necessary to take numerous policy decisions at the last minute, and feed these into the technical configuration. From an operational perspective, this represents poor management. From a practical perspective, delaying numerous CRM policy decisions makes the change-management programme fraught with unnecessary pressures.

The manager's task is to ensure that as many relevant decisions are made as soon as possible. This will make the implementation process far smoother, and give users time to become familiar with the changes as the solution arrives. Assuming accurate mapping between CRM functionality and organisational change, and movement towards the CRM vision, the need to take these decisions should be identified at an early stage.

The role of the process professional

The earlier section on 'process' introduces the idea of 'the process professional' – managers responsible for one or more processes, in addition to a part of a silo area or even a complete silo. The requirement is to create some 'cross-organisational process professionals', and make these managers responsible for helping to achieve the initial configuration. Subsequently, these managers should take ownership of specific processes and, therefore, the day-to-day operation and administration of the CRM solution.

The manager, as process professional, should take responsibility for the process, and specifically:

- Understand the definition of the process, including the aspects relating to cultural change
- Define any changes, and ensure these are documented to the required project standard
- Support the initial configuration of the process, including field and data definitions
- Support managers with adjacent processes, to ensure the development of an end-to-end solution
- Manage the ongoing development of the process, through the pilot stage, and through to the live environment

For example, a 'process manager' would take responsibility for

- *Enquiry handling process*, which might include working with external lead-handling agencies, marketing, sales people, and customer service (assuming a 'closed loop' environment.)
- *The telemarketing process*, from seeing that the organisation's segmentation strategy works in practice in the telemarketing environment, through to the processes of interaction between telemarketing and field sales
- *Forecasting process*, from working with marketing to ensure the use of the correct external reference data, to helping managers understand the new forecasting environment, and reporting tools, and any relationship between forecast accuracy and commission schemes
- *The customer complaint-handling process*, ensuring that the Key

Account Manager's views on the complaint process are taken into account, and that marketing understand the data collection opportunities they should be exploiting concerning complaints

- *Running marketing campaigns*, and ensuring the implementation of a 'closed loop' process. This requires a cross-organisational process team encompassing any group involved in creating a campaign, executing the campaign and campaign reporting – i.e. a group much wider than the marketing department
- *Field-service visits* – allocating, monitoring and reporting on field service visits, and the process of ensuring a relationship between field-service reports and product development (i.e. capturing what customers say about products to drive product development)

Thus, using the concept of 'process professionals' different managers take responsibility for different parts of the CRM business

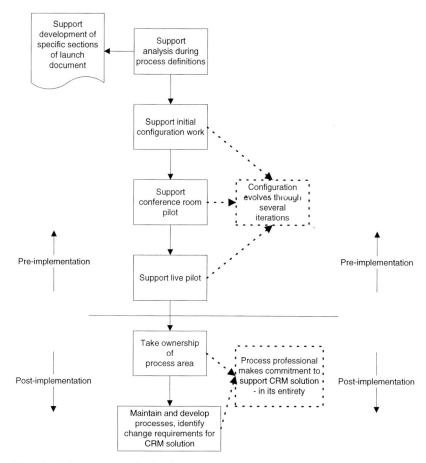

The role of the process professional

process and solution, specifically as it relates to the cross-organisational nature of CRM. The advantages of this approach are that:

- The workload of matching system and process is shared around the organisation
- Managers get a better understanding of the way in which the solution operates, as an end-to-end process
- Managers are better prepared to use the solution in the live environment, having been directly involved in the development phases
- Those developing the solution have a point of contact, within the business, to which they can address all issues relating to the development of the solution relevant to a particular process
- The CRM project manager, with good lines of communication to the business managers, is more likely to hear about any critical changes to the business that may affect the CRM solution

There are however disadvantages to this approach. The project involves more people from an earlier stage, and requires greater co-ordination than working with a small core team. For example, this approach needs greater co-ordination to bring together the thinking of a much wider group of managers. In addition, managers unfamiliar with thinking in process or system terms may take some time to get up to speed with these concepts. On the other hand, managers have to take ownership of 'their' solution. Therefore, the sooner they are involved the better. The diagram above illustrates the role of the process professional.

Solution ownership

The concept of the process professional highlights the importance of having the solution 'owned' by the managers of the business. With ownership should come a sense of responsibility, towards both the part of the solution used, and to the overall success of the CRM project. After all, the solution should belong to the sales, marketing and customer-service managers. These managers are presumably responsible for what happens in their departments. This responsibility must extend to their part of cross-functional processes, and to the solutions selected by the organisation – i.e. the CRM solution.

Piloting the CRM solution

The pilot stage should test a working configuration. It is not the place to develop the configuration. And, assuming the project team follows the processes as outlined in earlier sections with regard to process definition and ownership, the pilot will have basic components for success.

It is important to define the meaning of the term 'pilot'. The easiest way to do this is to identify what a pilot should not be:

1. A pilot is not the time to give users an opportunity to decide if they do or do not want to accept the CRM solution. a) This is a decision for the management team and b) it is pointless leaving this decision to such a late stage in the project.
2. A pilot is not the time to find out that the chosen software solution is not going to meet user requirements. See 1 above.
3. A pilot is not the place to find out what requirements the users have; if this is happening at such a late stage there is something wrong with the project-management process.
4. A pilot is not an opportunity to wage war with the saboteurs of the CRM project.

So if a pilot is none of the above, what is it?
Simply put, a pilot is a time to fine-tune the solution, before rolling out the solution to the users. It is a time to check that what is expected to happen does happen. The definition of 'solution' encompasses far more than the software solution. 'Solution' in these terms includes all the components of the CRM strategy, including:

*   The configured software
*   Data migration routines[20]
*   Data integration routines
*   Business processes
*   Reports and the process for extracting data from the solution
*   Training courses
*   Cultural change programmes
*   The work required to position managers as 'CRM coaches'

Two types of pilot

Because of the complexity of the CRM project, and the fact that CRM operates across the organisation, there is a requirement to run two types of pilot. Firstly, a 'conference-room pilot' and secondly, an 'operational pilot' or 'live pilot'.

The conference-room pilot
As its name suggests, the conference-room pilot happens in a conference room, rather than in the working environment. There are three reasons for running a conference-room pilot:

---

[20] Both pilots require data, and the section which follows covers this topic.

1. To reduce risk
2. To pilot the training concepts
3. To provide extensive use of the solution in a short time-scale

1. Risk reduction

It is pointless exposing even small groups of users to a solution without first undertaking some controlled test. The conference-room pilot tests processes without the risk of any adverse impact on either customer relations or the reputation of the solution within the organisation. A well-controlled conference-room pilot paves the way for a more general pilot in the live environment.

2. Piloting the training

The section on training demonstrates that CRM training is about more than simply showing delegates which buttons to press; in consequence getting the training completed is a complex task. The training material must be set in the context of the overall solution and therefore take account of operational and cultural changes. The conference pilot is the first iteration of developing the training programme.

3. Extensive use

The conference-room pilot should replicate a complete period of use for the user – perhaps a complete quarter. And it will do so in a fraction of the elapsed time. This is necessary because many CRM users, especially field-based users such as customer-service engineers, sales people and account managers, only use the CRM solution for short periods of time. In any single week, they might use the solution for just a few hours. In a conference-room pilot these users can run processes continuously – far more than they can in a field pilot.

Running the live pilot

Pilots are 'resource-intensive', and require similar resources to when the project goes live. In particular, to run either conference-room or live pilots, managers must have in place the following:

Resources required for the pilot

- Hardware
- The configured CRM solution and a CRM 'road-map'
- Migrated / integrated data
- Training / cultural change resources
- People resources – process managers, management champions, etc.
- Pilot objectives and a means to gather feedback

Pilot resources – Hardware

The pilot is the time to test the solution, *as it is to operate in the live environment*. Therefore, for the pilot, it is essential to use the same hardware – at least the same specification – as planned for the roll out. For reasons of false economy and expedience some organisations attempt to get through the pilot using lower specification hardware, simply because it is available. Using different hardware for the pilot is not a true representation of the live solution and generally below-specification hardware will be reflected in the performance of the solution.

Pilot resources – The configured CRM solution and a CRM 'road-map'

Managers must decide on **how much of the solution to make available**, and at what stage of the project various processes are to be integrated within the solution. Whilst this decision comes at an earlier stage it is a decision with wide implication for the pilot. **The general rule is to provide the right level of functionality to generate enough immediate payback at an early stage of roll out,** but not too much, for fear of overwhelming the users.

Additionally, the pilot must allow for completion of specific processes across the organisation.

There must be no gaps where users are not on-line, and because of this they interrupt the completion of a cross-organisational business process.

Providing a Road-Map

It is essential to provide a clear 'road-map' of how the system is to be rolled out. A 'road-map' is a simple guide that shows the business processes managed by the CRM solution (and, in practical terms, managed by the software element of the solution), and when they are to come on-line. Until both pilots are complete, it is not possible to be exact about when the rest of the solution is to be available. Planned dates will be known, but not exact dates – these depend on the success of the pilot. Therefore, managers should make the dates in the road-map 'approximate'.

Given below is an example of a 'road-map' for the CRM solution. In this example, the road-map illustrates the roll out for the customer-services element of the solution. In practice, it is necessary to create a road-map for each process area.

The following illustrates as an example a 'road-map' for the roll out of the Customer-Service element of a CRM solution:

Phase 1 ~ 1st Quarter 2001
Go live with the following:
- Basic customer file, to record new incidents (excluding level 1 incidents)

- Acknowledgement letters / e-mails
- Automated transfer of incidents to account managers
- Management of incidents entered on the web site

NB Continue to use existing systems for inbound 'phone calls to Customer Service

Phase 2 ~about 2nd Quarter 2001
Go live with the following:
- Interface to customer master file
- Recording of level 1 requests
- Reporting modules
- Work-allocation modules
- Computer / telephony interface for automated call handling

Phase 3 ~about 3rd Quarter 2001
Go live with the following:
- Knowledge database and intranet integration
- Interface to product master file
- Interface to stock-management system
- Interface to data warehouse
- Use of customer-service data in campaigns module

Pilot resources – migrated / integrated data

Data is the lifeblood of the solution. With the right data the solution comes to life and provides utility to the users – the opposite having the opposite effect – i.e. the wrong data leads to a lifeless and valueless solution. To be successful the pilot will require a copy of live data.

In any case, the software routines for extracting data and the interfaces to other solutions need piloting, and this work should be an integral part of piloting the solution. (The work on the data must, of course, be done in good time to provide live data for the pilots.)

Pilot resources – training / cultural change material

The reason for including 'cultural change' in the pilot is to remind managers that the roll out and the training are all part of a wider cultural change, i.e. a change towards a more CRM-centric organisation.

As part of this move towards a different culture, managers should prepare both the CRM training and the training for 'managers as CRM coaches'.

In practical terms, running pilot training provides an opportunity to identify how easy or how difficult it will be for users to learn the solution and also to identify any issues relating to cultural change.

Pilot resources – people

The following people resources are necessary for the pilot:

- The process owners / process managers
- Senior-level sponsor, ideally a direct representative of the CEO who can champion the solution
- Vendor technical specialists – especially to fix any immediate problems there may be with the software or network
- The end users *representing the cross-organisational processing being piloted*

Pilot resources – objectives, and a means to gather feedback

It is essential to begin both pilots with a precise understanding of the pilot objectives. In addition, everyone involved in the pilot should be aware of the feedback expected from them.

Given that the solution is to support various CRM processes, it makes sense to establish pilot objectives ***per process*** and gather feedback in a similar manner. Bringing a document together which outlines both objectives and feedback should be a straightforward task – the material for the pilot objectives coming from the initial process specification, suitably adapted to provide feedback. An example follows:

**CRM pilot
Process(es) : Enquiry processing, and 'closed loop' lead handling**

Summary of process objectives:

One-touch lead handling to allocate a new enquiry from any source (e.g. web, e-mail, fax, 'phone) to the correct sales channel.

The solution must ensure that:

- Customers and prospective customers receive acknowledgement of their enquiry within 1 working day
- All enquiries are in the hands of the correct channel (e.g. major account sales, field sales, telemarketing or distributors) within 2 working days
- Ensure this process does not create duplicates on the database
- Lead-handling statistics and lead-location statistics are available as per specification
- The outcome (closed loop process) of each enquiry is known within 4 weeks

Experience shows that gathering feedback is essential, but must be easily achieved and explicitly relevant to the pilot users. The responsibility for gathering feedback should be delegated to the process owner (i.e. the 'process professional') – someone who has a considerable stake in ensuring the success of the project.

The following recording format should suffice for 90% of the feedback. The other 10% can be gathered directly, through hands-on observation, by members of the project team or other feedback routes:

Summary

Many CRM projects do not get beyond the pilot stage. Of those that do, many emerge as watered-down versions of the original CRM vision, or bounce between so called pilot and roll out, as managers struggle to complete the tasks outlined within this section.

The main reason for failure, at this stage, is that managers fail to heed the advice to 'make haste slowly' during the pilot stages. Sufficient time is required at the pilot stage to ensure that a number of things happen. Clearly, the solution needs testing in its entirety to be sure that, come the roll out, the solution will meet user needs to complete the relevant end-to-end processes in a true cross-organisational manner.

However, the pilot is the time to transfer ownership of the solution, and ownership must shift from the CRM project team to each CRM process manager. From the pilot onwards these managers and end users must drive the project forward.

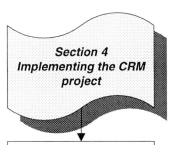

**Section 4
Implementing the CRM
project**

Project phases
Why CRM projects never
end, the different
approaches required for
each stage, and the core
project threads

**Mapping the CRM vision
to the project**
Putting the software
element into context,
producing a project launch
document, defining and
signing-off user
requirements

**Configuring and piloting
the solution**
Building a prototype, and
planning and managing
both conference room
pilots and field pilots.
Managing pilot feedback,
piloting the training
solution

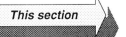

This section

**Data migration and
integration**
The operational challenge
of CRM data, finding and
using suitable data,
making sure everything
goes smoothly

Data migration and data integration

Working definitions for 'data integration' and 'data migration'

It is necessary to provide some working definitions for this topic. The following are non–technical definitions for both integration and migration.

Data integration is concerned with making data held in one or many other systems available in the CRM solution. Data integration makes sales history available to those that make the sales and manage the accounts – i.e. marketing, sales, and customer service, from sales order-processing systems.

Data migration is concerned with taking data from existing databases, and bringing this data together in the CRM solution. For example, taking the 'data' a sales person has about customers and prospects and making this data available to all, via the CRM solution.

In an ideal world, organisations would have perfect, all-encompassing enterprise-wide systems working from a single database and requiring no integration or migration. However, a need for data integration and migration comes about because of the piecemeal approach to developing IT systems, adopted by most organisations. This piecemeal approach arises because of the different priorities that companies have for different parts of the business, leading to phased development of database-related solutions. In addition, a further reason for CRM projects to require extensive data migration and integration is merger and acquisition activity between companies. By definition, merging organisations must bring together their data sets and systems to create a unified organisation.

How to fail at implementing a CRM solution

Managers wishing to fail at CRM or sabotage a CRM project need look no further than 'Data' to find the *weakest* link in the CRM project.

To fail, simply remove or corrupt the data. This makes the solution virtually worthless. In this case, 'corrupt the data' need not involve some form of technical corruption. As damaging as technical corruption is, far more can go wrong with CRM data than the technologists can manage on their own.

'Corrupt' data includes data that is:

- Out-of-date data
- Inaccurate data
- Data in the wrong place / at the wrong time
- Duplicate data

How to succeed at implementing a CRM solution

Managers wishing to succeed at CRM need look no further than 'data', to find the ***strongest*** bond holding the solution together.

If the solution provides sound data, the value of the solution becomes immediately apparent to all users. Not surprisingly, with sound data there is more chance users will subsequently use the solution. In this case 'sound data' means data that is both accurate and data that is relevant. Combining accuracy and relevance brings the reward of utility.

Accurate and relevant data is data that is:

- Up-to-date and kept up-to-date
- Accurate to an agreed level of detail
- In the correct place at the correct time
- Data which is not duplicated

At face value, the challenge of data in the CRM project should not be too difficult to overcome; it should simply be a technical challenge to migrate many databases into a single database, and / or integrate data from one or many systems to the CRM solution. See diagram below.

However, as with many aspects of the CRM project, the challenge has as much to do with cultural and operational change as it has to do with 'technology'. In addition, because of the perishable 'time-value' nature of data, timing is crucial in managing the transition from using data in one system or solution to using the data in another. (The 'time value' of data relates to the last time the data was verified, and the rate at which it changes and requires updating.)

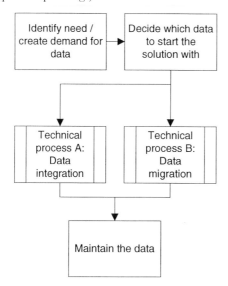

Starting the solution with the correct data

The 'challenge of data' encompasses three aspects:

- The technology
- Time value
- Cultural change

These three aspects, technology, time value, and cultural change, need setting in the context of the CRM project process, and the aim of starting the solution with the correct data.

Identify data need / create the demand for data

Asking a group of managers what data they need to improve productivity in sales, marketing and / or customer service produces a list that is either very long or very short.

These extremes come about because managers, generally starved of data on which to run their business, either:

a)   Have little expectation of what data they could have or could use. These managers produce a very short list.

or

b)   Have unrealistic expectations of the CRM solution. These managers produce a very long list.

Ideally, the need for data comes from the process analysis and drops out of the several iterations required to develop an understanding of the needs of users, as discussed in an earlier section and represented in the diagram below. Additionally, the provision of data should follow the scoping / prioritisation exercise.

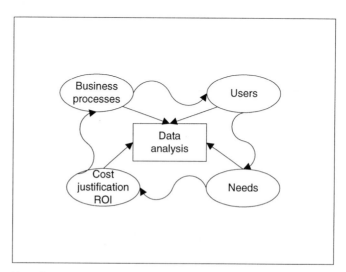

Data and iteration

It is important to guard against the extremes of having either too much data or too little data. Too little data and the CRM solution is generally of limited value. Too much data and the job of migration or integration can swamp the project either technically or culturally.

Determining which data set should start the solution

Data has a cost. Not only does data 'cost' in terms of the real cost of finding, cleansing and integrating the data, but also in terms of managing and maintaining the data, once it is in the solution.

A balance is required between the availability and cost of the data, and its value to the users. A useful approach is to map the data onto a matrix, as indicated below. Users can then see the options against the cost and benefit of the data, and subsequently make an informed decision about their starting point.

An approach to data selection, indicated in the diagram below, considers data in terms of its availability on the axis 'available now / available at a cost'. This axis is mapped against the utility of the data, as

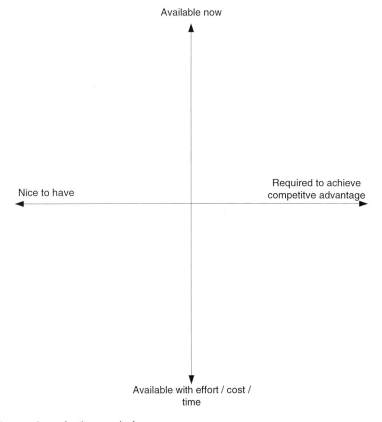

Diagram data selection matrix A

'nice to have' / required to achieve competitive advantage. Producing such a matrix helps to focus managers when faced with demands for either too much data or too little data.

Typically, managers take a phased approach with data, and a typical and often recommended phasing might be across 4 phases as illustrated.

Because users new to CRM can only cope with so much new data, this 4-phased approach favours the need to gradually acclimatise users to CRM. Additionally, the approach avoids the effort of providing expensive and 'nice to have' data, before users are familiar enough with the solution to be sure of their data needs. The iterative development process, mentioned previously, continues beyond the initial implementation, so it is possible to add more data at a later stage.

Data, and the impact of CRM on managers

Through CRM, managers should change their work practices. In the main, this requires a change from being mainly fact finders to being managers acting on information taken from the CRM solution. Achieving this shift is partly done by making sure the right data is in the CRM solution in the first place. A pre-requisite is, of course, that the CRM solution provides useable management reports, based on the data held within the solution.

Without providing good management reports, managers are unlikely to attribute the CRM solution with sufficient value to warrant their support, thus risking the overall success of the project. This is an often-overlooked requirement, with managers promised management reports as part of some later phase. Sadly, this 'later phase' offers little to the disillusioned manager who, by this stage, sees nothing of particular value in the CRM solution to help him in his work. It is therefore essential to start the solution with reports in place

Technical issues associated with integration and migration

Two issues complicate the integration of data between multiple systems.

1) The need to map data from different systems; to create and subsequently maintain a co-ordinated view of the data generally requires a complicated process that sits between one of many systems. And these systems serve quite different purposes within the organisation (see diagram below).

2) The need to integrate and maintain systems from different manufactures which may change at different times and in different ways.

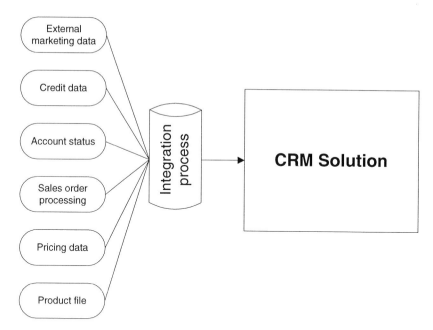

These two issues introduce a high level of complexity, and any issue associated with data integration is not to be underestimated in terms of both technical and operational complexity.

The diagram illustrates some of the complexity of providing an all-encompassing CRM solution. Data from many different systems needs pulling together, to provide a workable view of what is happening in the real world, for the CRM solution users. Moreover, the data is ever-changing and processes need to be in place, to keep the view current.

The place of the 'Portal' solution

One approach that helps to remove the complexity of integration is to use a 'Portal'. The term Portal means 'Gateway' i.e. as a gateway into data and information. A Portal simply 'sits' over all systems and allows the user to have a view of data from any system, presented in a browser environment. In doing so, the user still enjoys the functionality available in the underlying system. The Portal is still relatively new technology, although the popularity of such an approach is increasing.

The dangers of poor integration

A 'straw poll' of 10 mid-sized CRM projects reveals that, out of 10 projects, 7 were severely delayed due to problems with data integration:

- Technical failure of the integration solution during the pilot, delaying roll out

- A decision being taken to adapt and change one side of the integration, delaying the supply of essential data to the CRM solution
- Conflict between the CRM vendor and the supplier of the other solutions or
- Severe data incompatibility and users then having to re-key data into the CRM solution

Technically, what is the problem, and what goes wrong with data integration?

Bringing data from several systems together is a bit like trying to use an automated language translator. You put in a word or phrase in one language, and hope that it comes out with the same meaning in the other language. In theory it should do so; however data, like the syntax of a language, has its own complex rules which may not succumb to a direct translation.

The following are the main problem areas associated with data integration:

1. The mapping issue – mapping database records and codes
In an ideal world, the data held in one system matches the data required in another system. Alternatively (another ideal), both systems use the same underlying databases.

As an example, consider the apparently simple task of mapping a 'customer master file' found in customer service with the customer 'contact file' used in the sales part of the CRM solution.

The sales department typically sells to sites unknown to customer service. Customer service may know only about sites concerned with delivery and invoicing or using the products or services sold. Meanwhile, the sales order-processing system does not store details of the sites that the sales team visit within a company. The problem is to bring the data together so that, overall, the utility of the data remains high. The integration process needs to identify and maintain the status of each address type, to avoid confusion when using the data in either sales or customer service. Adding to the complexity is that the integration process must accommodate the need to change and maintain the data by different groups of users.

2. The timing issue
Data integration routines may be run as a batch process, or online process. With the batch process, data integration occurs at a regular frequency. In an online process, as the term implies, the data integration happens whilst the user is 'online' to either system.

For an example of the 'timing issue', consider the integration between sales history data held in the sales order-processing system, and the account-management part of the CRM solution. In order to provide data that is meaningful to the CRM users, the data needs integrating such that the result makes chronological sense. There is little point in showing the account manager's last quarter's sales, coupled with the previous quarter's invoicing, credits and returns, alongside year-old stocking data, for example.

In addition, bringing data from different systems with different time references is difficult enough. Sometimes adding to the complexity is the need the customer has to view the data relative to the customer's account periods, rather than the suppliers. And, of course, customers may have different time references. It is no wonder that many account managers still rely on their customers for a breakdown of sales and such reliance is definitely not good for CRM.

3. System maintenance / upgrades and changes
All systems require maintenance, be it upgrades or fixes to the original solution – or fixes to the problems introduced as a result of an upgrade. Changes to either system are likely to require a change to the integration solution, which in effect sits between each system. In system terms, the integration 'solution' is the weak link in providing data from one solution to another solution – especially when changes are being made.

Because of the issues listed above, and the general reason of 'complexity', managers should be wary of agreeing to complex integration solutions. Before proceeding, they should be confident in both the integration solution provider and the relative stability of the integrating solutions. However, complexity is not sufficient reason to avoid the problems of integration. To implement CRM to the standards now required to achieve competitive advantage, managers frequently have no other option but to integrate.

Integration and the ERP providers
The fact that the integration element of the CRM solution is such a weak link is good news for the ERP providers. These providers know that through their UBS solutions they avoid the risk of having to implement systems with critical elements out of their direct control (that is, the critical integration elements, which they may be forced to share with other vendors). Removing the need to integrate removes this high-risk aspect of the CRM solution for the ERP vendors.

Practical steps to avoid problems with data integration
The following checklist should help managers avoid major problems in integrating to other systems:

Keep it simple – try at all costs to avoid overly complex data integration. Overly complex means taking data from one or more systems, massaging it, presenting it to another system, and returning it re-massaged back to the original system. In such a scenario, unless 100% confident of success, try to simplify the process, or alternatively, downgrade the solution instead. Less complex integration sends data just one way and simply maps existing data items. Simple integration avoids restructuring the data and brings it lower risk.

Be aware of the volumes of data involved – in particular, understand the time required integrating the data and running the integration processes. Managers need to understand the likely operational impact of the integration solution and the associated risk. The reality may be that what looks fine on paper is going to take an age to run, and therefore is totally impractical.

Consider data integration the weakest link in the technical solution and assume that at some point, for short or long periods, the data integration solution may not be operational. Take this pessimistic view and design the CRM solution to be self-standing, to work even in the event of the integration solution failing.

Be wary of time estimates – it is extremely rare that the technologists can deliver the integration on time and within budget. This is not a criticism of the technologists, simply a reflection on the complexity of building what are – almost by definition – unique software programs, and programs that must coexist between two ever-changing targets. Therefore, allow considerable margin for slippage in this part of the project plan. Additionally, ensure a good period for testing the integration element.

Assess the longevity of the integrating systems. Producing the integration solution is time-consuming, high cost and generally high risk. The risk that the investment is to be short-lived is directly proportional to the longevity of the systems sitting either side of the integration solution. Managers should therefore be aware of likely changes which may affect the stability of the overall solution. It is essential managers know of any pending changes to either solution well before making integration an essential element in the CRM solution.

Despite its complexity, fragility, and high-risk nature, integration is an essential part of achieving competitive advantage in many CRM solutions. It is rare to exclude integration from the project, if the CRM solution is to provide a good ROI and meet the 'roles' outlined in the earlier section. Therefore, the message about integration should be clear.

Yes, integrate the CRM solution with the other systems within the business, but make haste slowly and tread very carefully, giving due regard for the risks involved.

Data Migration

Data migration is concerned with bringing together disparate databases used throughout the organisation to populate the CRM solution. 'Database' is a very broad term. In the world of CRM, database could mean the data from a first-generation SFA system or from a marketing database. 'Data' can also mean the random jottings of a thousand sales records cards, prised from the grasping hands of the sales team.

There are 3 main issues to be wary of regarding data migration:

1) *Data ownership*. Managers and / or individuals may be reluctant to give up what they see as 'their' data, and have their data merged for the common good of the organisation within the CRM solution.

2) *Bringing data together at the right time*. The timing of the data migration must fit the timing of the roll out of the solution. If this does not happen, users will have the worst possible combination – a brand-new system with either no or incomplete data.

3) *The diversity of data in use and diverse data formats*. The diversity of 'databases' in use, and therefore requiring migration can vary. In a project with very wide scope this could easily involve data held in:

- Numerous 'Contact Managers'
- Spreadsheets
- 'Home-made' databases
- First-generation SFA / similar solutions
- Call-centre applications
- Customer-care applications
- 'Back-office' systems
- Paper record cards
- Backs of envelopes in glove compartments
- Lead-handling agencies
- Channel partners
- Other external service providers

Data migration is a complex part of the CRM project. It is rarely practical nor beneficial to migrate every piece of data into the new solution. What is required, of course, is the right quality and quantity of data migrated with minimum hassle, and with maximum efficiency and effectiveness. Easy to say, but far more difficult to achieve.

Technically, what is the problem, what goes wrong with data migration?

From a technical perspective, the problems of data migration are similar to the problems of data integration. The difference, however, is that migration is generally a one-off process, whereas integration is an ongoing process. With migration, the technologists have more scope to manipulate the data in whatever way they may choose, as long as the result is acceptable. At the same time, migrating the data into the brand-new CRM solution assumes a degree of data cleansing. This data cleansing is required to avoid the problem of having old and tired data, in the new and invigorating CRM solution.

The specific problems of data migration centre on the following issues:

1. Locating data

The same company may appear in all databases – but each database record may show a different address and different contacts – or rather (and far worse) the 'same' address and contacts, only spelt differently. The migration problem is how to manage this 'difference', and create a sensible single database with which to initiate the new CRM solution. The initial hurdle is to view the data, and decide which department(s) data to include within the migration process.

Additionally, the format of the data may be critical in determining whether it is possible to bring the data into the new solution. The critical factor is that users may require access to data held in the manner of the old solution. If it is not possible to present data in this way, then the initial value of the new system appears limited.

For example, 'sales-visit reports' held simply as Microsoft Word Documents may be difficult to import into the new CRM solution. To avoid manually attaching the sales-visit reports, sales people may need to refer to the 'old' solution, whilst using the 'new' solution. Equally, if marketing, sales and customer service are to share a common database, perhaps integrated with the accounts solution, it is necessary to have just one set of company and contact details – see point 2 below, dealing with duplicate data.

For efficient data migration, it is necessary to determine which department has which data, and then assess how to migrate the data. A straightforward approach to assessing the data situation is to work from the analysis phase, where the analysis phase reveals the need for the data in the CRM, and compare this with what is available within and outside the organisation.

Shown overleaf is an example table to illustrate where and how the organisation holds data. Once the table is complete, managers can review the situation and determine how the data is to be migrated, what data is to be migrated, and what cultural issues they may face during this process.

2. Dealing with duplicate data

Are 'Mr Gone Away' (provided by the lead-handling agency) and Mrs 'Goneaway' (held in the marketing database) one and the same? Is Eastbourne really in West Glamorganshire, Scotland, and is there such a town as 'Not sure will add later'? To these practical data questions, there are several software solutions available for helping with formatting addresses and de-duplicating data. These solutions help to add data such as postcodes, and automatically compare database records to find and deal with duplicates.[21]

Managing this process is vital to the success of the project. Get it right and users will hit the ground running, safe in the knowledge they have the right data, in the right place, at the right time, ready to implement the CRM strategy. However, without meaningful data the CRM solution will not provide the necessary utility, and managers will not appreciate having to spend the first few months of using the CRM solution sorting out badly prepared data.

3. Timing the migration of the data, to mirror the roll out of the solution

Having worked out the *process* of migration, it is then necessary to work out the *logistics* of the migration.

Predominately, the logistics means planning the *on-going* migration of the data from the old system(s) to the new solution. Unless, of course, the implementation is to take a 'big bang' approach – in which case, there is just one migration to do, all in one go.

In practice, this means ensuring an ongoing process of data migration carefully timed to match the roll out of the new solution. For the project manager, this means ensuring technical support is in place, to carry out and manage the data migration / roll-out process.

Practical steps to take, to avoid problems with data migration

Explain the problems of migration to all the users and why everything must work 'like clockwork'.

Get all the resources in place well before the roll out starts to get up to speed.

---

[21] Examples include 'Quick Address, see www.quickaddress.co.uk., and E4 selling systems; for de-duplication solutions, see http://www.e4.co.uk/dedupe.htm. Other similar systems are available from other vendors.

	Marketing dept	Sales dept	Customer service	Accounts	Channel managers	Product marketing	Lead handling agency
Company Name and addresses	Enquiry file held in MS Access	Contacts held in ACT! and Goldmine, plus paper	All held on customer service system	Held in two system - sales and accounts	Use Excel spreadsheets for all data	Have company data in data analysis tool	Use Siebel system for recording leads
Contact details	In MS Access - added for every enquiry so duplicates	As above	As above	Hold only 1 account clerk name	As above	Old file of contact types	Do not store contacts, once passed through
Activity data - meetings, reports, complaints etc.	Not held	Stored partly in ACT! etc, mostly on paper	As above	N/A	File visit reports using MS Word	Store product interviews in bespoke solution	Do not store contacts, once passed through
Potential business needs	Separate file, held in MS Excel	Stored in forecast system (bespoke)	N/A	N/A	Uses Excel for forecasting	As above	Do not store contacts, once passed through
Previous business	Receives file from Accounts	Held in Word - one document per account	N/A	In accounts system	Held in Word - one document per account	Uses datafile in Cognos system	N/A
Account objectives and strategy	N/A	Held in Word document (where completed)	N/A	N/A	No formal or agreed process	N/A	N/A

Data migration, showing location of data

Document everything so that, whatever happens if some data does end up in the wrong place, it should be possible to back-track and correct any errors.

Be aware of anything that may change to impact on the migration process.

Summary, data migration and integration

Without the right data from the very start, the CRM solution is likely to flounder. Managers will question the very viability of the project, and be forced to continue using their old sources of data. With the right data, managers immediately see the utility and value of the CRM solution.

**Section 5
Change management
and CRM training
Contents**

Change management
A model for the change
management program,
and the challenge and
specifics of cultural
change

CRM Training programs
Background and logistics,
plus the anatomy of a
CRM training course.
Course guides and ideas

**Section 5
Change management
and CRM training**

Change management
A model for the change
management program,
and the challenge and
specifics of cultural
change

This section

CRM Training programs
Background and logistics,
plus the anatomy of a
CRM training course.
Course guides and ideas

Cultural change and training

This section outlines the format for CRM training, and introduces a model around which to discuss the cultural-change aspect of the CRM implementation.

A simple model for cultural change

The model used to frame the change-management programme brings together a number of concepts introduced in earlier sections. These concepts include the drivers for CRM focusing on customer retention. The model then considers the need to re-examine the 'silo' structure, so prevalent in many sales, marketing and customer-service operations.

To create a meaningful model it is often necessary to simplify what may be an extremely complex situation, and this is the case here.

In this case, the simplification uses the assumption that:

- Organisations have customers taken from them forcibly by a predatory competitor
- Organisations lose customers through their own neglect

Simply put, customers are either snatched or we drop them.
A quick examination reveals that:

- Customers 'move' between the silos in an organisation at the command of the supplier – not because they enjoy it
- As customers move from one silo to another, the organisation may accidentally drop them
- As customers move from one silo to another, predatory competitors snatch them, either completely or as part of a 'deconstruction' strategy

The diagram over summarises this model.

The model for cultural change excludes any references to other market influences, such as the four, six, eight or however many Ps there are now. Here, the focus is on what the organisation does wrong as an organisation – not on what the organisation produces or how it prices or how it promotes, etc relevant to the rest of the market.

The cultural-change model for CRM is to focus on the following issues:

- From a cultural perspective, how can the organisation stop 'dropping' customers as they move between silos, or stop predators from snatching them?

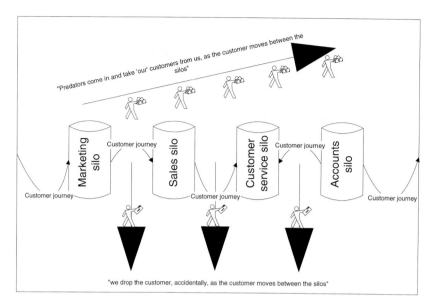

The competition 'picks off' customers as the customer moves between silos in the organisation – or they are accidentally dropped by the organisation as they move between the silos.

- What impact will the introduction of end-to-end sales, marketing and customer-relationship management processes have on the organisation?

Culture, and the challenge of cultural change

'Organisational culture' is of course the subject for many other references, as is the management of the change of organisational culture. It is not therefore the intention here to go into the depths of the subject. However, there is a requirement for a simple model of 'organisational culture' against which it is possible to frame the CRM implementation – or rather, the changes to culture required to support the implementation.

In its simplest form, culture is seen as a set of shared:

- Ideas
- Beliefs
- Traditions
- Values

In our case, it helps to think of 'organisational culture' existing at two levels. Firstly, within each 'silo' and secondly, across the organisation as a whole. Thus, a picture of organisational culture, relative to sales marketing and customer service, can be represented as in the following diagram.

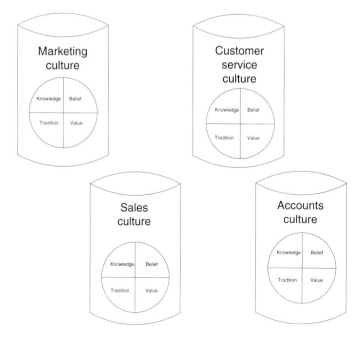

A 'typical' feature of culture in sales, marketing and customer service is that 'different' culture exists within each silo. Consider the concept of 'different cultures' per silo against the drivers for CRM, and the specific challenge of change management emerges. *Well-implemented CRM should bring all departments and cultures in line.*

Achieving such cultural change requires managers to implement the end-to-end processes using the terms of reference identified during the analysis stage. For example, explaining the aims of the solution in terms of the:

- People
- Process
- Technology

Model, and explain the rationale for implementing each end-to-end process. Achieving such an explanation is possible through an effective CRM training programme.

**Section 5
Change management
and CRM training**

Change management
A model for the change
management program,
and the challenge and
specifics of cultural
change

CRM Training programs
Background and logistics,
plus the anatomy of a
CRM training course.
Course guides and ideas

This section

Training

This section considers the details of the CRM training programme. The section starts with a framework to explain CRM training. It goes on to consider practicalities such as when and where to carry out the training, the training agenda, and training schedule. It also tackles the important issue of training 'middle-level managers'. The section concludes by considering the need to link training on the CRM solution, to other training programmes within the organisation.

Background to training and the CRM project

Using the stage of project model as an indicator, it is clear that training sits between two main stages of the CRM project – implementation and achieving ROI and cultural change. Reaching the training stage is a significant turning point in the project. At this point, the 'attitude and approach' of the project team may shift from a pragmatic operational focus on getting the implementation details right, to a consistent reinforcement of change – as indicated in the diagram below.

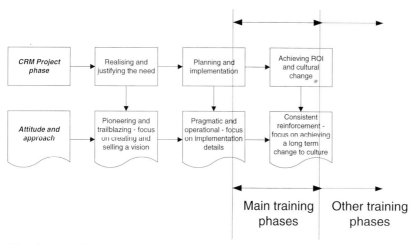

Training, attitude, and approach

The reality of training, and linking the vision of CRM to the desired reality of CRM

The training phase is not the 'end-game' for the CRM project, and it is too naive to assume that, left to their own devices, users will achieve the required return on investment and visionary change. Now, more than ever, users need considerable help and support:

- Training is required to create a direct link between CRM vision and CRM reality

- Training is required to apply the data bond that makes CRM stick
- Training is required to change 'hearts and minds' – which is the essence of the CRM implementation

Take training seriously and all the efforts of the past months are more likely to pay off. Pay lip service to training, and the project team will have to revisit and revisit and revisit the training issue.

Preparing the training program – a framework for CRM training

The diagram below provides a framework for CRM training. The diagram shows the link, through training, between CRM vision and CRM reality, and the need to see training as far more than simply showing users 'which buttons to press'.

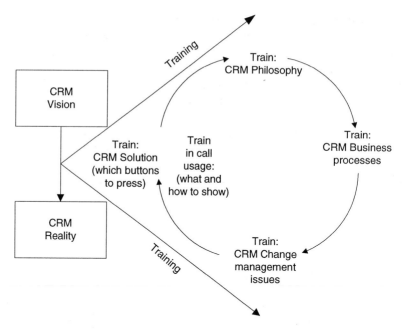

CRM Training concepts

The main CRM training concepts:

CRM philosophy – train users to understand the cultural change the organisation is aiming for

CRM process – train users to understand the business process affected by the CRM solution

Change management issues – train users to understand how their roles will change, as the CRM solution goes live

Which buttons to press – train users to understand how to get the most from the system element of the CRM solution

The above assumes the implementation of a CRM strategy within an established organisation. Consider the situation in a new start-up. In a start-up situation, the process would be far more straightforward and require far less effort in respect of the 'soft' cultural change training elements (since, by definition, the start-up is still developing its culture).

This is a further indication of the potential for new players to make swift advances through a well-developed CRM strategy. New players bring with them no legacy systems, and no need to make cultural change. This means that training and implementation can move at a far quicker pace.

Bringing the training requirements together

The training components should be brought together from a very early stage in the project process. Therefore many elements of the training programme should be in place even by the pilot stage, and the pilot stage should be seen as an opportunity to 'pilot' the training, in addition to the other components of the solution.

As the project 'iterates' it way through to fruition, the training requirements are revealed. And as they are revealed, the training

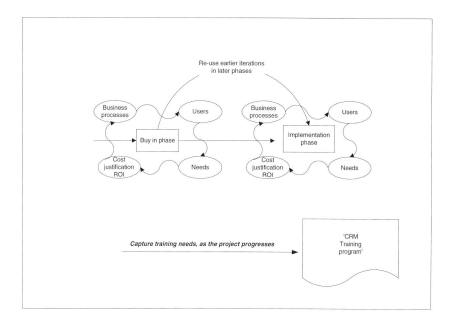

organisation needs to capture them and position them within the training programme. The process is similar to the process of capturing data items, and other aspects of the project through the various iterations, as identified in the diagram overleaf:

Bringing the training requirements together, as the project progresses, places the project team in a far stronger position to plan for the practicalities of the CRM training. These include planning the logistics of the CRM training sessions, and the components of each course.

Logistics of the initial CRM training

These include:

- How to structure the training groups
- The length of each course
- In what sequence the training should happen
- The impact of CRM training on the normal workload, and when to train / implement

How to structure the training groups

Having said that CRM should break down the 'silos' within organisations, it appears contradictory, for training purposes, to group users by function. The 'road-map' and philosophy of CRM say that a better grouping is by *business process* rather than business function.

The reality, however, is that bringing groups together by business process is rarely possible for logistical reasons. For example, forming a group to represent the 'Account Management' process, would involve combining a training group such as:

- Sales
- Customer Service
- Account Managers
- Marketing
- Product managers
- Accounts

The group would have some processes in common, but their differences would be greater than the processes they work on collectively. To overcome the problem, they would ideally come together for training in those parts of the process on which they work together. Then thereafter separate to work on their individual areas. Again, this is rarely practical for logistical reasons, and would be extremely time-consuming and expensive to organise.

A compromise solution is to group by *function* for training, but have available business managers who understand the end-to-end processes, as they impact *across* the organisation. Coupled with well-briefed trainers (see below), this compromise helps to break down the 'silos' with regard to end-to-end processes, and still allow functional training to continue.

A practical approach to achieving a sensible grouping is therefore to:

a) Identify which modules / process of the CRM solution each functional group must use, and produce a grouping accordingly (the traditional functional groups of marketing, sales and customer service, for example)

b) Identify the areas where processes overlap between the functional groups. For these overlapping areas, schedule a cross-function briefing within the training programme. For example, allow marketing to explain their use of CRM to sales, sales to explain their intentions to marketing and so on through customer service, product managers and all associated functional groups

The 'cross-functional briefing' would show for example:

*   Why customer service need sales to enter call reports, and how sales can benefit by the data customer service collect on the service organisations' operational performance
*   How, post-CRM, marketing will run campaigns for specific sales regions, and how sales will receive sales leads via the solution
*   Why marketing and sales need to take care in how they interpret the end of quarter sales figures, and how accounts gather the data – perhaps presentation by someone from the finance department

How long each course will last, will depend on the following factors:

*   How familiar the users are with software and using PCs
*   The complexity of the solution
*   How many cross-functional issues need addressing
*   How quickly the group might be expected to learn

In practice, the duration of a CRM course is rarely less than a day, and rarely more than 2½ days. The upper duration of 2½ days is generally set more for logistical and learning reasons than as a reflection of what there is to learn. In any case, over 2½ days the ability of adult learners to continue to pick up new concepts reduces dramatically in this type of training.

Section 1 Course introduction	
Course introduction, video from CEO (see 'anatomy of a CRM training session' below.)	Allow 15-30 minutes total.
Introduction to CRM solution	Allow 15 – 30 minutes total.
Where CRM fits into the company's business process and philosophy / culture.	30 minutes – open discussion on change management issues and CRM vision.
Section 2 CRM solution and business process	
Learning to navigate the solution. Basic rules of the road for navigating the software solution.	Depends on complexity. Allow 1 hour minimum to 1 hour 30 minutes for average complexity, 2 hours for complex solutions. In this time, users should learn how to move around the software application – although not to the level of achieving any specific productivity improvements.
Understanding how to navigate the main modules of the solution.	Allow minimum 30 minutes to 2 hours *per module*. A module being, for example, the 'Company details file' 'Contacts file' 'Service management module' 'Campaigns module' and so on. In this time, users should understand slightly more than the basics of each module they are to use.
Matching the main modules to the business process.	Allow additional minimum 15-45 minutes *per module* to introduce how the modules map onto the business process. In this time, users should start to understand how the CRM solution will support the business process and improve productivity.
Cross-functional processes.	Allow 30 / 45 minutes, for each presentation from cross-functional departments. As an example, in this time customer services should present to sales, sales should present to marketing, and so on.
Section 3 Change management and cultural change	
Training exercises to demonstrate how CRM impacts on the wider organisation.	Allow from 30 minutes to 3 hours, depending on seniority of delegates, and complexity of solution. In this time, users should understand the wider implications of the CRM solution, as it supports the 'end-to-end' processes – i.e. how CRM will be breaking down the silos in the organisation.
Cementing the change.	Allow 1 to 3 hours to enable delegates to complete exercises using the CRM solution, as if in the live environment. In this time, users should be comfortable about applying the CRM solution to their working situations, and may use a live database rather than the training database.

Users need enough time to be confident of switching to the new solution, and enough time to accept the vision the organisation has for the 'reality of CRM'.

When considering the duration of a course, managers needing a rule of thumb to calculate course duration should consult the table on previous page. The table provides a method to assess the duration of a CRM training course, with an outline of the main topics.

The example below indicates the timing for a 2-day course, using the guidelines from the above table.

Example scenario: CRM training course for Account Management team. The team are implementing a CRM solution to address threats from an e-commerce start-up, and enhance relationships with their global accounts.

Day one	
Section 1	
Introduction, including video from CEO.	20 minutes.
Presentation of CRM solution.	15 minutes.
Company CRM philosophy, and management discussion.	30 – 45 minutes led by Senior Account change Manager's manager.
	Sub total 1 hour to 1 hour 20 minutes
Navigating the CRM solution	
Section 2 Main modules: ● Company file ● Contact file ● Activity file ● Sales analysis ● Relationship management and record sharing	Various exercises to set these modules into the context of the business process. 5 modules in total, allow remainder of day 1 – approximately 1 hour per module. NB more time for follow-up learning, scheduled for day 2.
Day two	
Section 3	
Revision, main modules and the business process.	'Day in the life of' exercises. Designed to connect CRM solution with new CRM business processes, plus further training on the CRM application. Allow 1 hour.
Cross-functional presentations.	Presentations by representatives from: ● Marketing – how marketing will use CRM to plan 'lifetime value' campaigns

continued

Cross-functional presentations. continued	• Customer Service – how customer service plan to report on account service calls, via the CRM solution, to account managers
	Total 1 hour 15 minutes.
'Workshop exercises'.	Total 1 hour. How the company vision for CRM will impact on the Account Management team.
Application revision.	Use remaining time (approximately 2 hours) to ensure delegates understand how to use the solution and are accepting of the company vision for CRM.
End of course.	Some delegates may require additional application training; schedule as required.

In what sequence the training should happen

The sequencing must help to ensure that as the roll-out progresses, end-to-end processes can ideally come online without pause – for example, to allow a user group to complete their training before they can participate in a particular process.

In an ideal world, the project team avoids any significant pauses in the roll out. Failing that, it is necessary give clear instructions regarding the timing of any changeover from old procedures and processes to new procedures and processes. In particular, it is essential to be clear about any interim measures that may be required.

What aspects of the solution to train

Allowing users to grasp the basics first may necessitate running both 'basic' and 'advanced' training courses. However, if this is necessary it is a small price to pay, being preferable to confusing delegates by cramming too much into one course – and then having to repeat the 'basic' training again.

Before scheduling an 'advanced' course, consider that if users start using the system often the perceived need for such a course disappears. In other cases, 'advanced training' is delivered in the workplace, without the need for formalised training. For example, in some cases line managers handle the advanced training in a coaching capacity, or the internal help desk provides it on an ad-hoc basis in the guise of support.

In summary, the training sequence should ensure:

1) That managers are trained first, and treated as a special case (see below)
2) That the software element is phased in, to avoid overwhelming delegates

3) That the roll-out and training sequence ideally mirrors the flow of the end-to-end business processes across the organisation
4) That the sequence of training takes account of what is going on in the wider organisation (see below)

Taking account of existing workloads and targets

One of the additional factors to take account of is that those involved in the training are usually very closely targeted and monitored. Most significantly, sales personnel have carefully negotiated targets. Generally, targets assume so many days' business activity over the target period. And, in the world of sales, marketing and customer service, there is surprisingly little time for actual selling. Allowing for holidays and non-selling days, for example days taken up with meetings and other training days, a typical sales person is likely to manage fewer than 200 selling days per year – calculated as follows:

---

365 days in the year *less*
104 weekend days
35 days' annual leave including bank holidays

226 balance remaining *less*

12 days for monthly meetings lasting total one day
12 days for average one day per month product training
12 days where not a lot happens – since everyone has at least one 'off day' each month

190 business days remaining

The CRM training will take an average of 2 days, plus travelling time, time to get up to speed, time to check data, and time to become familiar with new processes and procedures. Optimistically, this takes a total (including training) of 4 days. Pessimistically, the total is 6 days, including CRM training to be deducted from an already short selling-year because of the CRM roll out.

As a percentage, 4 to 6 days represents between just over 2% and just over 3% respectively of the business time available. The CRM solution should easily provide efficiencies that recoup such an investment – but probably not in the quarter or even the year in which the implementation goes live. Which department therefore has to pay for the opportunity costs of this?

For example, until they have the solution, sales people and their managers may not immediately agree that the returns will accrue as planned. A sales person, sales manager, or sales director who is just over 2% to just over 3% away from target may not willingly take an immediate risk that the CRM solution will give an immediate payback.

Anatomy of a CRM training session

The anatomy breaks down into 3 sections as summarised below.

A – Personnel involved in the training
B – Technology requirements
C – Training material

Personnel involved in the training

CEO (or rather, a video presentation by the CEO or similar)

The role of the CEO at this stage (or similar high-level influencer within the organisation) is to help the CRM team add importance and weight to the training and legitimise the roll out of the CRM solution.

The recommendation is to use a video of the CEO for this purpose – in preference to the live version. The problem with the CEO's live version is that logistics dictate that he or she cannot possibly be available at every training event to endorse the project.

A video of the CEO delivering the 'CRM message' provides a consistent message to each delegate at each showing. In addition, of course, the video version has the added advantages of being available for presentation in more than one place at a time, and is available on demand.

The message the video is to deliver

As an introduction to a training course, delegates will accept about 10-12 minutes of video (much beyond this length of time, boredom sets in – which quickly converts itself to cynicism). On the basis that a good listening rate is about 300-400 words per minute, the text of the video needs to be about 3,000 to 5,000 words.

In these 10-12 minutes the message to get across is:

- That the senior management team endorse the use of the CRM solution, and that they too will be users of the CRM solution (give examples)
- That CRM brings opportunities for competitive advantage (give examples)
- That CRM protects the organisation from competitors (give examples)
- That CRM is about to change how the organisation operates (give examples)
- That using CRM is not an option – it is mandatory
- That the training is important
- That there are specific objectives for the training, and delegates

are to achieve these objectives as directed by the trainer (give examples)

If the CEO decides it would be a good idea to use the opportunity of the CRM training to get another message across (whilst there is a seemingly captive audience for it) *resist this pressure at all costs.* At this stage, the project does not need a watered-down half-hearted message about CRM, shared with some other message. What the project needs is a robust, enthusiastic, and knowledgeable endorsement of the project, one dedicated to the CRM solution.

One or more trained trainers
If the training were only about *how to use a piece of software,* the training task would be straightforward. Simply show a few screens, show a few icons and some keyboard short cuts, and send the delegates on their way.

However, *how to use the software* is only one element of the training. The more complex elements include:

- The relationship between the CRM solution, and the change to the organisational culture
- The relationship between the CRM solution, and changes to the business process

It is essential therefore that the trainers are able to multi-task. The trainers must present CRM as a solution to the problems faced by the organisation – as well as a software system.

How many trainers?
A trainer should be able to manage a group of about 8 delegates. The basis of this assumption is that in a training session, at any one time:

- Half the delegates – i.e. 4 – are quietly working on the training task and don't require any specific help
- 2 delegates are struggling, but able to work on with a little support from the trainer
- The remaining two delegates require the close attention of the trainer

One trainer should therefore be able to manage the workload. The ratio of 1 trainer to 8 delegates assumes the availability of a representative from the business, to support the trainer on an ad-hoc basis, plus a technical support person. A further assumption is that the delegates include some 'process professionals', these 'champions' being exposed to the CRM solution, perhaps through the pilot, and / or at earlier stages of the project. It is important to spread these champions evenly, across as many training courses as possible.

A manager to support the trainer

Since 'middle-level managers' are an essential part of selling the CRM vision to users, it makes sense to include these managers in the training, as the roll out progresses. Their presence is required for at least two reasons. Primarily, it is to support the roll out and help sell in the CRM solution. Secondly, it is to provide support to the trainer. This is because however well briefed the external trainers are, there will be some company-specific situations arising which require a manager to deal with and explain to the delegates, in a way that an external trainer cannot.

The ratio of managers to delegates need not be the same as for external trainers, i.e. it is not necessary to have one business manager per 8 delegates. Depending on the complexity and cultural change task, one business manager per 3, 4 or even 5 courses, running concurrently, should suffice.

Technical support personnel

The advice regarding technical personnel is to assume that what can go wrong will go wrong – especially if there are no technical personnel available on-site. Having technical support personnel available on site for all training courses may prove to be logistically difficult, and incur additional cost. The additional cost could include the internal cost of having IT personnel at the training and / or the direct cost of paying for external resources. External resources can include technical representatives from the CRM solution vendor, and / or personnel to manage and support the server.

The cost of on-site technical support during training is generally well worth paying. The alternative of not having technical support during training is to run the risk of either having to re-schedule a complete training session or re-schedule sections of training excluded due to system failure.

Providing technical support – remotely

It may be possible to provide technical support remotely. For example, holding the training in a hotel does not necessarily mean that the technical resource must be on-site at the hotel. Remote support is viable as long as:

a)   The technologists can go online to fix things when they go wrong
b)   There is someone at the training venue to explain (at least in semi-technical terms) to the support team what went wrong, and work with the technologists to put it right
c)   There is sufficient faith in the local IT infrastructure that remote support will continue to be an option for the duration of the course
d)   There is enough time beforehand to test a-b, above

PCs, servers and network connections

The whole paraphernalia of technology needed to support the CRM solution needs to be in place, tested, working and supportable, to enable the training to operate effectively. At face value, it should be simple to pick up and put down this paraphernalia of technology from one location to the next. Server(s), routers, PCs, monitors, network connections should theoretically all be instantly connectable, anywhere, providing some basic infrastructure exists.

In practical terms, this means that when booking training venues it is vital to allow enough time beforehand to set up the infrastructure. A day before the event is fine. The morning of the event is not acceptable. Plus, of course, remember to budget accordingly if the venue charges for the set-up time.

The CRM Solution

Stating the obvious, every user needs to have access to the CRM solution for the training.

In the in-house environment this is not difficult to achieve. More difficult to deal with is the set-up of numerous laptop PCs, and the creation of a database for training purposes for field-based users.

Problems arise when users are to have the CRM solution loaded onto their *existing* laptops, for the training and subsequent roll out. Even a well-organised IT department cannot be expected to know the state of every laptop in every customer-service representative's car, sales person's brief case, or account manager's hotel room. Therefore, some considerable preparation is required.

Ideally, these field-based workers should be able to arrive at the training session, deposit their laptops for a few minutes (perhaps during the introduction to the course) whilst the technologists load up the application on the laptop.

The problem is that in many cases the application may not load. Or, the loading takes more time than is available at the start of a course, especially taking into account that 40 / 60 / 100 users may be training at the same time, all of whom need some attention to their laptops.

Aside from the time required to load the application, simple technical problems arise, such as a lack of space on the hard drive, or users forgetting to bring their detachable CD drives with them (usually required for software loading). Whilst these problems are easy to overcome, they cause frustrating delays. With a little up-front effort these delays are avoidable.

Therefore, it is necessary well before the CRM course to hold an internal audit of the state of each laptop. For example, disk capacity, operating system, modem set-up, operating system configuration, etc. The technologists should advise the project team of the specific issues they face in loading the software. The project team then needs to schedule a laptop audit, to take place well before any training. Users then need telling what they can and cannot change on the laptop, pending the loading of the new CRM solution and attendance at the training.

Establishing a training database

The solution without a database is of no value for training purposes. If there is no data, users will find it extremely difficult to make the connection between the solution, the business process, the cultural change, and the whole philosophy of the CRM strategy.

Ideally, users should have a mirror image of the database they are to use in the live environment. This serves the purpose of providing realism without risk. That is, the data will be realistic to the users, but users can safely make errors in the training database. Towards the end of the training, users should then have the option to switch to the live database, once they have sufficient confidence to do so.

Supporting software such as Microsoft Office and related applications

Microsoft Office is an important component because CRM vendors develop their CRM products to integrate to it. For example, for users wishing to create a letter using data in the CRM solution (data such as name and address), it makes sense to utilise MS Office to create that letter. Accordingly, it does not make sense for the CRM vendors to recreate such Office-style software in the CRM solution.

Such integration is of tremendous benefit to the CRM community. CRM vendors no longer need to create word processors, report generators and the like, as integral parts of their CRM solution (as they needed up to even a few years ago.) As long as the CRM vendor's solution integrates to MS Office (or similar), everything in this area will be fine.

If the CRM solution relies on MS Office, as many CRM solutions do, when is the training provided for those users unfamiliar with MS Office? Moreover, the same applies to those yet to be exposed to the operating system, and for that matter using PC software generally.

For most internal users already using PCs this is not an issue – assuming they are like 'most' office-based workers the world over, i.e. they already use MS Office (or similar). The problem is not with 'most users'. The problem is with a very special cohort, those who have not had the opportunity of exposure to MS Office (or similar) or the delights of the Windows operating system or PCs in general. And, in the world of CRM, this potentially represents a very large group indeed. Field-based personnel have spent the last decade outside the office – quite literally, out in the cold and away from the 'white heat of technology'.

Through no fault of their own, these field-based cohorts will be the last ever to suffer the problem of IT exclusion.

The impact of this 'low-tech' cohort on CRM training

What this means to CRM training is that CRM project managers, at least for the next 5 years or so, must be sensitive to this as an issue – and consider the training requirement accordingly. Otherwise, the CRM training will be short-lived, and users will need to go away and find a 'PC appreciation course' before tackling the CRM solution.

From a practical perspective, CRM project managers should identify whether the chosen CRM solution relies on other applications, and arrange training accordingly. It is essential to complete this training in advance of the CRM training. The training must provide users with sufficient confidence to use MS Office (or whatever). Plus, of course, to use the PC and associated parts of the operating system.

Training components directly related to the training course

Trainer's notes

Assuming the project calls for more than one trainer, there will be a requirement to produce some 'trainer's notes' to serve as a briefing document to external trainers. These will be required for the train-the-trainer course necessary, of course, in preparation for the full roll out of the solution.

These train-the-trainer notes need to explain the rational behind the project and behind each exercise, and demonstrate to the trainer how the course designer expects the delegate to learn from the various exercises within the course. At the same time, the trainer's notes should highlight where, in the light of experience at a pilot, delegates are likely to have difficulty with the software and what the acceptable work-arounds are.

In addition, trainers need briefing about the questions they might expect from delegates. This brief should include the range of topics that the business manager at the training session is to answer, and what questions the trainer is expected to answer.

Training material

The training material should contain the following, in this order:

Section 1 – an introduction

- An introduction to the course, with a preface by the CEO – an extract from the introductory video (see above) is ideal for this purpose
- A summary of the learning objectives for the course
- An outline as to how the course topics fit with the business process

Section 2 – using the solution to meet the aims of the CRM project

- Training exercises bringing together process, cultural change, and CRM application
- Self-assessment exercises, to allow delegates to test their own progress and understanding as the course progresses
- 'Cheat-sheets' on the main concepts associated with the key business processes

Section 3 – the impact of CRM on the wider organisation

- Extracts of the presentations, made by the cross-functional managers
- A 'road-map', outlining any future additions and scheduled changes to the CRM solution

The training exercises should guide delegates towards what they should achieve – but not necessarily provide a keystroke-by-keystroke guide to using the chosen software solution.

Delegates should learn which 'buttons to press', and how the CRM solution relates to their business process and the strategic aims that the organisation has for the CRM solution. Each exercise should be followed by a self-assessment, enabling the delegates to check their understanding as the course progresses.

CRM Training and managers

CRM projects succeed or fail according to the degree of commitment shown to the project by managers. In addition, the role of the middle-level manager changes dramatically because of implementing a CRM solution. This combination of holding a pivotal position in the project, and facing a considerable change to job role, singles the manager out to require specific and different training from his subordinate users.

There are 3 main training-related issues to consider, with regard to middle-level managers

- Timing – when to train managers, relative to other users
- Course content – and how this varies from the content provided to other users
- Support – and how to help line managers become 'CRM coaches'

Timing

It is essential to train middle-level managers first, i.e. before training those they manage. Insist, as an immovable principle, that managers take time out to get a complete understanding of the CRM project and CRM solution. Such understanding must happen before exposing the managers to rigorous questioning about CRM from those they manage, and well before they are expected to help the organisation achieve a substantial ROI from the CRM investment.

Armed with this understanding, managers are in a position to guide their workers to ever-increasing levels of productivity, with the new CRM solution. Without this understanding, managers struggle. They struggle to explain to their subordinates what CRM is about, and they struggle to explain how to use the new CRM solution – even for the most basic tasks.

In the 'worst case scenario', managers duck out of training and assume that the new CRM solution is something of an operational tool. They assume they can get others to push the buttons of the CRM solution for them – the necessary reality could not be further from the truth.

CRM management training – course content

To help managers dispel any thoughts about operating like 'big brother' and promote CRM as a tool to improve management as well as operational efficiency, the management training must cover three main areas:

1. The 'basic roles' of CRM (see earlier section)
2. How to use data to manage in the CRM environment
3. The importance of the manager's role as CRM coach

Area 1 of CRM Management training – basic roles of CRM

Managers need to understand the 6 main roles of the CRM solution, i.e. the role of CRM being:

- Customer-centric – not 'supplier-centric'
- Predictive
- Directly supportive of customer retention
- Measuring (the right things)
- Supporting processes
- Measuring customer value

The aim is not to turn these managers into academics or CRM specialists. What is important is that all managers have at least some appreciation of CRM, beyond the practical application within the departments they manage.

Remembering that the course under discussion refers to managers, have the training organisation structure some sessions to evaluate the above roles, in the context of the organisation. The earlier needs analysis work, and justification for the investment in the CRM solution will provide plenty of material to support this management training.

Area 2 of CRM Management training – how to use data to manage in the CRM environment

Successful managers in the CRM environment, particularly those in marketing and sales, have long perfected the art of management through gut reaction, i.e. management with minimal data.

Having such minimal data is in stark contrast to managers in other areas of the business, such as those in manufacturing, finance, and accounts. Many of these managers (though certainly not all) enjoy the luxury of full data-sets, complete with the ability to analyse their part of the business.

Similarly, CRM should provide managers in the CRM environment, finally, with all-embracing data-sets, and with the same opportunity to analyse data from numerous perspectives. Moreover, from implementation forward, managers in other departments will have an increasing expectation that accurate data will form the basis of reports from sales, marketing and customer-service managers. Especially at board level, will those directors frustrated with the lack of supporting data have an expectation of ever- improving management reports, via the CRM solution.

The training requirement therefore is to train managers to:

1. Proactively use the data held in the CRM solution, to meet the ROI aims of the project
2. Meet the increased expectation of their colleagues, regarding management reporting

A prerequisite to achieving these training objectives is to incorporate the original reporting expectations. That is, the reporting expectations detailed by managers, during the needs-analysis phase of the project. Managers must be able to produce reports in training that they will use in the live environment.

With data, managers can move quickly to the process of finding out what is going on in their departments using the CRM solution. Therefore they should move quickly away from the past, where 'finding out' occupies 80% of available management time, and move quickly to a position where 'doing things' represents 80% of their activity – see earlier section.

Area 3 of CRM management training – the manager's role in the CRM implementation

Already identified is the pivotal role of the manager in the CRM implementation. In practice, line managers make or break CRM projects. They do so through the quality of their practical approach to the implementation, and the overall backing they give to the project.

Managers need telling about the importance of their role in the CRM project. They need telling that, to make CRM work, it is imperative that as 'line managers' they demonstrate their full backing in three ways:

- The managers' general attitude towards the CRM philosophy and solution
- The managers' specific understanding of how and why their subordinates are to use the CRM solution
- Using the CRM solution to improve the role of the manager as coach

The managers' general attitude towards the CRM philosophy, and solution

Once the project moves to the point of training managers, there can be little room for a negative view from managers. By this point, the CRM implementation is for real, and managers must back the philosophy.

Specific understanding of how subordinates will use the CRM solution

Whilst managers are themselves unlikely to press all the buttons on the CRM solution, they still need to understand what processes, within their domain, the CRM solution is to support. Not only that, managers need a good understanding of processes across the wider organisation, especially where the managers' department may – perhaps for the first time – interact with another department in a different 'silo'.

Therefore, management training must not neglect operational aspects of the solution. In particular, each manager should have an understanding of what their subordinates should be doing with the CRM solution, and be in a position to brief them accordingly.

Using the CRM solution to improve the role of the manager as a coach

Managing in a world of limited data, dominated by the gut-reaction school of management, makes the job of coaching subordinates especially difficult. For example, sales personnel and account managers are frequently measured solely on the 'output' side of their effort – i.e. sales revenue. As a crude measure, 'output' takes little account of the input to sales – inputs such as enquiries, account potential, opportunities with group companies. In addition, simply measuring output fails to measure how effectively the individual manages each process.

Post-CRM, the 'manager as coach' can see clearly how his or her subordinates perform at different stages of the process. For example, the CRM solution should reveal how well or otherwise sales people manage opportunities and exploit potential and use their time. The solution should show the effectiveness of sales presentations, how well or otherwise account managers build relationships and track associated companies, and how effectively marketing personnel design, manage and measure campaigns. Additionally, the CRM solution should provide comparative analysis to compare the performance relative to a process of one person vs a group average or similar metrics.

With over a decade of CRM projects it is now clear that managers can profit from the management reports from the CRM solution if they use these reports to coach for improved performance. Managers should be looking to the CRM solution to provide an understanding of the effort, outcome, and rewards associated with each significant process.

As an example, consider the customer-service task of retaining existing customers, where those customers signal their intention to defect. The CRM solution should highlight:

The effort. In this case the effort needed to retain each customer group. For example, 'phone calls, letters, incentives, discounts and reductions in margin.

The outcome. In this example, the degree of defection, i.e. all business defects are retained or a percentage of the business defects are retained.

The reward. The net gain per period resulting from stemming the defection.

Armed with such an understanding, managers can coach their subordinates to greater levels of effectiveness, and at the same time seek and implement process improvements. If managers gather this data, but fail to use it to coach, they are missing one of the most valuable aspects of the CRM solution.

Integrating other training with the CRM solution

Relationship between skills-based training and the CRM solution

The concern is to keep the CRM solution in step with the skills and ability of the users. Achieving this, requires some connection between skills-based training, and training in the use of the CRM solution.

Without a connection, users are liable to implement their new-found skills using solutions aside from the CRM solution. A practice which may lead to the eventual demise of the CRM solution.

Skills-based training in these departments includes training for:

- Customer-service representatives on how to pacify an angry customer
- Customer-service representatives on how to find new opportunities, within the accounts they look after
- Sales people, learning about 'key account management' and the importance of 'life-time value' in the account relationship
- Sales people learning how to qualify their prospects, and make maximum use of their time
- Marketing, training to understand the intricacies of international segmentation strategies
- Marketing, learning the theory about optimised campaign management, and strategies for rejuvenating a campaign, mid way through the life of the campaign

The training outlined above will give a better return if managers understand how to use their business tools to convert classroom theory into business reality. Therefore, somewhere in the training process, it is necessary to connect the CRM solution with skills training, as in the examples below:

Based on the training courses outlined above, users would need to have a good understanding of the CRM solution regarding:

- Customer services to access a knowledge database containing a wealth of knowledge, to pacify even the angriest of customers
- Customer services to run an automated process to qualify an existing account customer as a 'new' customer, for an alternative range of products – and then automatically generate a sales lead for the relevant sales person
- Sales people to use the CRM solution to extract data to make 'life-time value' calculations, and share the account-management process with other managers
- Sales people to run activity reports, and analyse how they could make better use of their time
- Marketing to use the CRM solution to plan, execute, and monitor international / multilingual campaigns

The main requirement is to avoid managers returning from training motivated to put into practice new-found skills, but unable to do so because of limitations within the CRM solution.

Summary

It may be an old adage, but it is correct to say, especially in this case, 'training is an investment – not a cost'.

The requirement to train users in all three areas of the solution – the software, the processes, and the vision – should be self-evident. Without training, even the best-designed solution will probably fail – or at least fail to get a good return on the investment. In addition, one cannot expect users to connect intuitively and overnight with a CRM project that has taken months to evolve. Users need showing in detail what CRM really means to the organisation and they need training time to understand what they see.

To achieve good quality training, the production of training courses and material begins at the earliest possible stage. This connects training within the project at the pilot stage, in good time for the roll out. But training cannot stop after the roll out. Remember that, as the solution changes, there may be a requirement for top-up training, just as there will be a requirement to train new users as they join the organisation or change departments.

CRM training should be 'institutionalised' within the HR induction process. It should be a part of any other training members of the organisation receive on joining – especially where the use of the CRM solution is connected with other training such as 'Account Management' or 'Customer Service'.

Section 6
The global or trans-
national implementation
Contents

Globalisation
Is globalisation of CRM
worthwhile, and should
globalisation equal
standardisation?

The difference
What are the specific
differences the CRM
analyst should look for,
in the global CRM project?

The global or trans-national implementation

Introduction

As the world gets ever smaller, firms increasingly need to consider their CRM strategy on a global or at least a trans-national basis. Firms operating in more than one country need similar systems throughout, and the ability to get a corporate-wide view of the business. Equally, it is increasingly likely that the trans- national or global company has trans-national or global customers. These customers expect similar levels of customer service, similar marketing approaches, and even similar account-management strategies from whichever country's operation they deal with. All these factors point to the need to implement a global CRM solution.

The trans-national or global CRM implementation brings with it some very different situations to the single country implementation. These situations present an entirely new set of challenges for the CRM project manager. Not least are the differences of language, culture, and variations in existing procedures between operating divisions. In addition, it is common to find that every country location already has a mini-CRM strategy or at least customer / contact strategy; perhaps a strategy that is part way through implementation or one that is working well (as far as the local operation is concerned). By necessity, these local initiatives must generally give way to the central initiative, giving rise to a whole area fraught with political and similar problems. Not least, the CRM sponsor must prove that the centralised solution will outperform the local solution, something often extremely hard to do.

Achieving success in this challenging CRM environment needs a careful consideration of the issues facing the CRM project. Therefore this section starts by examining what is driving global CRM and the concept of 'difference' between requirements in different geographical locations.

The section goes on to consider the system issues and concludes with tips and ideas regarding the pace and direction of rolling out a trans-national or global project.

**Section 6
The global or trans-
national
implementation**

This section

Globalisation
Is globalisation of CRM
worthwhile, and should
globalisation equal
standardisation?

The difference
What are the specific
differences the CRM
analyst should look for,
in the global CRM project

Why bother with Global CRM – should globalisation equal standardisation?

Rarely do firms have global procedures for marketing, sales, and customer-service activity; however, global CRM can realistically be a project that enables the organisation to 'think global – act local'.

What global CRM should be about is standardising only where it makes economic sense to do so and, at the same time, leveraging the differences between local operations, to achieve a better overall return.

Too often, local managers view global projects as the sponsoring location's attempt to get every country working in the same way, i.e. the way the sponsoring location works. Firms see global CRM as head office wanting to standardise, wanting to make it easier *for itself to manage* – rather than as a project about directly improving the productivity and effectiveness of the local operation, and leveraging global opportunities.

Approaching global CRM as a centrally imposed philosophy is generally a recipe for failure, literally on a global scale.

The starting point, therefore, is not to approach 'global CRM' as though it is a 'Global CRM project' with the aim of standardising everything in every sales, marketing, and customer-service department in the corporate empire. Rather, approach the project as a means to an end, the end being one in which the organisation:

1. Minimises the cost and maximises the benefit of the organisation's CRM infrastructure, including system support and maintenance costs. *Because generally one system is cheaper to maintain than many*

2. Measures efficiently the progress towards the desired CRM position. *With global CRM, comparisons across geographical boundaries become possible, and thereby measurement towards global objectives becomes easier*

3. Meets any current or future requirement that trans-national / global customers have for trans-national or global trading. *Increasing opportunities to retain larger, globally focused accounts, through providing improved levels of CRM-related services around the world*

4. Provides and leverages competitive intelligence across the organisation. *Reducing the time and cost of gathering competitor intelligence, and putting it to work for the benefit of the whole organisation*

5. Leverages 'best practice' in terms of CRM practices, CRM process, and CRM system management, around the organisation. *Quickly sharing profitable ideas, which because of*

common systems can quickly be implemented throughout the business
6. Provides the ability for employee mobility, in a world where national boundaries shrink and employees are deployable in one of many countries. *Increasing the ability to transfer employee knowledge, and may help retain key personnel*

And once the organisation is in agreement as to why it is undertaking this high risk, high cost, difficult and time-consuming project, it is possible to move ahead – though still on the basis of making haste slowly.

Section 6
The global or trans-
national
implementation

Globalisation
Is globalisation of CRM
worthwhile, and should
globalisation equal
standardisation?

This section

The difference
What are the specific
differences the CRM
analyst should look for,
in the global CRM project

Vive la différénce!

The jobs of providing customer service, of carrying out marketing, and of selling, are carried out in a remarkably similar way throughout the world. After all, there are only so many ways to do similar work. Providing the CRM solution supports several ways, the chances are it will be suited to the needs of every country location. Nevertheless, it is important to highlight any significant differences in process between countries, and this requires a close examination of what is actually going on.

"Aah yes... but here, we do things differently, but it doesn't work like that here, never has done, and never will ..."

Even in today's global business community, if you ask someone in the north of a continent to adopt the business practices of the south, the likely answer is the one above. If you try the same, east to west, the answer does not change. The challenge of global CRM is in determining if there really is a difference, and if the difference actually matters.

Differences between similar operations across different countries are likely to become apparent in four main areas:

- **The local legislative regime**
- **Different ways of using apparently similar distribution channels**
- **Cultural and linguistic differences**

There are other differences. However, on a 'search for difference', the four places listed above would be a good place to start.

The local legislative regime

Even within a seemingly unified Europe, there are differences concerning the legality of storing and using data. These differences include variants on Data Protection acts. They also include rules about how a company may make unsolicited approaches to individuals or other companies. Different countries have different laws regarding the rights of employees; for example, how companies may monitor the activity of workers or store personnel details within computer systems. In addition, legislation differs in different industry sectors, especially in highly regulated sectors such as financial services and pharmaceuticals. Unions and similar Workers' Councils, too, have an impact on how the CRM solution should function locally.

Rarely are these show-stopping differences. In practice, though, a local manager who wants to keep a local CRM strategy and solution will argue otherwise. Local managers may argue that local regulations, along with the custom and practice of the local operating division, may make the implementation of the global solution impossible.

The reason for raising this point is not to discuss how to meet local and world legislative frameworks. The reason is to alert CRM project managers to the issue, to enable the manager to pre-empt the situation and ask the question of the local countries. This therefore forms part of the analysing the difference in needs.

Different ways of using apparently similar distribution channels

One of the driving forces for CRM is to enable the organisation to get greater control of the distribution channel, and improve the available channel options.

However not all countries use the channel in the same way. For example, the role of an 'agent' and the role of a 'distributor' differ between the northern and southern parts of Europe. In the US, channel partners have different expectations of service levels from manufacturers, than have their counterparts in Asia. In parts of the sub-continent, the role of agent is more of a 'go between', and the precise influence of an individual or group is very difficult to determine – and it is often desired to keep it that way.

What this means for the CRM configuration is that how relationships are expressed may vary country-to-country, region-to-region. Moreover, different regions have different interpretations of the meaning of 'getting greater control of the channel'. In practice, this difference requires the global project manager to check that the method of creating channel relationships, using the software element of the solution, suits all situations. In particular, the difference is apparent in the terminology used to describe partners and the like, and the relationships between firms. Where this really matters is in respect of global channel partners. As globalisation continues, the strategic advantage of understanding the role and performance of a channel partner in different countries is likely to grow. Ideally the global CRM solution will provide such an understanding, but only if the configuration permits. This requires the manager to be aware of any global requirements in the proposed configuration, and have an understanding of local needs.

Cultural and linguistic differences

Despite the speed of globalisation, cultural differences between countries will no doubt continue to exist.

Having said that, the trend towards globalisation in the business world leads to an interesting cultural phenomenon – that of the 'international culture'. This culture exists within multi-national corporations, alongside the incumbent national culture.

The international culture comes into force where workers from more than one country meet. Co-workers put aside part of their natural cultural differences, and the culture of the organisation prevails – i.e. the 'international culture', often heavily influenced by the origin of the organisation. Outside of this influence, the 'national' culture prevails, at the expense of the international culture.

The relevance of international culture is the importance of recognising cultural difference as far as it affects the *implementation of the CRM solution*. The fact that a Japanese manager behaves in a manner that is different from a Swedish manager or a Puerto Rican manager is interesting, but is it relevant to the *implementation of the CRM solution?* In this case, relevance means does the CRM solution need to function in a different way? If it does, then record the difference, if it doesn't, there is nothing to record.

The reason for highlighting this issue is to warn analysts to be on their guard. Analysts need to avoid confusing a cultural difference with a requirement to make the CRM solution operate differently. An experienced analyst plays this to his or her advantage, and uses knowledge of culture and the recognition of the 'international culture' to tease out the differences that really matter, and set aside those that do not. An inexperienced analyst becomes blinded by the cultural differences, and assumes that the Japanese manager, the Swede and the Puerto Rican all need vastly different solutions. This is rarely the case, the reality being that they use the same solution, but in the context of their own local culture.

One international company – how many languages?
In an ideal global CRM implementation, everyone involved, including the customer, would speak the same language. All of the solutions would be in the same language and use the same character formatting. All the 'look-up tables' (from which coded entries are selected) would be in the same language. All users would make their entries in the text areas in the same language. However, we do not live in such an ideal CRM world.

The need for a global CRM solution assumes that managers from different countries will use the solution and the data in the solution, either centrally or across the organisation. Otherwise, why bother to go global? If this is not the case, save the investment, implement one solution per company, and don't bother about bringing the data together.

However, assuming there is a need for multiple languages, at some point the organisation needs to decide on the preferred language for the solution – or to accept the need to have either multiple language versions or a hybrid. And this is a significant decision.

A single language may cost less and be easier to implement, but will it be practical? – especially in areas such as customer service or a call centre. In these areas, will users be able to manage in a language that is not their 'own'? Often, a single language is not an option in call centres or customer-service operations must have local versions of the solution.

Multiple languages, although more expensive, may solve the problem. But this adds to the cost. In addition, the multi-language version costs more to maintain, simply because of the need to support many languages. Some vendors and systems do allow for a hybrid – where parts of the solution are localised, and the remainder kept in a single language. This option also needs consideration.

The best advice is to work on the basis that the core of the system is to be in one language. From that, provide options for multiple languages based on specific modules; for example, for call centres, customer-care, marketing administration, where users are less likely to be familiar with the core language.

Summary

The global CRM implementation is probably the most challenging of all CRM projects. Noticeably, there are few successes in this area and many failures. The successful global CRM projects are characterised by their rigid connection with a corporate vision, and the ability of the organisation to overcome the technical requirement to wire up their global empire. The failures are characterised by the inability of managers within the organisation to agree on even simple things, such as the database structures, and common processes, and failure to overcome the technical challenge.

Do not undertake global CRM lightly. The benefits of wiring up the empire under one solution must outweigh the cost of implementing say 3 or 4 smaller solutions – and sharing only relevant data rather than the whole solution; for example, share data together for reporting purposes or share major global account intelligence.

However, as the cost of communications fall, and the number of globally-focused organisations rise, expect to see an increasing drive towards globalisation.

The CRM imperative – to establish industry sector standards for CRM

Recent events in CRM have been dramatic. Since this book was started, CRM has moved away from the niche and into the mainstream. Today, virtually every firm on both sides of the Atlantic is offering its services as an 'e-CRM' or 'CRM' vendor. An explosion of CRM centric thinking has occurred, and the manager's task made harder by the need to 'do something' in response to the focus on CRM, and a need to decide on which opinion or fashion to follow.

At the same time, it seems that the initial internet bubble has burst, and 'dot coms' are now largely out of fashion (i.e. at the time of writing the NASDAQ is hitting an all-time low). The respected analysts Gartner are reporting that by 2003 there will be 'but a handful of CRM firms', predicting that yet another shake-out will rearrange the technology aspect of CRM, and the ability of the technology to deliver to the manager's aspirations for CRM.

It seems that on the one hand CRM is the most important business imperative, ever. But on the other the technology available to deliver CRM looks increasingly confusing, and it looks like the technology aspect will be dominated by just a handful of players.

In this environment, and taking account of the preceding chapters, what is a manager to do? If there is one imperative, what is it?

Perhaps the most important step managers should take is to begin to define the 'Way Forward' for an organisation's approach to CRM, *relative to available technology and emerging sector standards for CRM*. This involves thinking about both business strategy and the use of appropriate technology at the same time. That is avoiding one-sided strategy definition where the business strategy is unsupportable by the technology, or the strategy is simply defined because of a preference for some sexy software or other.

But how do managers balance the two? How do managers define the right CRM strategy for their organisation – and make sure the strategy is achievable using **available** technology? And what of operational managers? – How do you get managers to agree a definition for CRM **and** implement the necessary processes to support CRM?

Based on the position of the CRM industry at this time it seems likely that the CRM community as a whole will move toward answering this question, led by a desire from managers to establish some order from the confusion which is currently CRM. The CRM community should provide an analysis of the adoption of CRM specific to industry sectors, and an analysis of how each sector approaches CRM. From this, managers and sectors can begin to define a 'generic' CRM process model for a particular sector. This will lead to the definition of strategy and essential CRM processes, which will form a benchmark for CRM within the sector.

Without this standard, CRM managers will struggle for some time with CRM as a 'grey' area, with little formalised structure. With it, CRM will reach further legitimacy and, hopefully, move away from a plateau position simply as a 'nice concept' and passing fad, and on to a position of standardised reality.

This implies that in the meantime organisations adopting true CRM models have the opportunity to define these standards and lead their peers towards the models they prefer, setting the standard for their industry sector.

And of course managers have an option in all of this – lead or follow, and that, finally, is the choice of the manager reading this book.

Index